Atlas of Travel Medicine and Health

University of Chester

Lorna Boyne

WIRRAL EDUCATION CENTRE
BC Decker Inc
LIBRARY
Hamilton • London
0151 604 7291

BC Decker Inc
P.O. Box 620, L.C.D. 1
Hamilton, Ontario L8N 3K7
Tel: 905-522-7017; 800-568-7281
Fax: 905-522-7839; 888-311-4987
E-mail: info@bcdecker.com
www.bcdecker.com

02 03 04 05/GSA/9 8 7 6 5 4 3 2 1

ISBN 1-55009-189-1
Printed in Spain

Sales and Distribution

United States
BC Decker Inc
P.O. Box 785
Lewiston, NY 14092-0785
Tel: 905-522-7017; 800-568-7281
Fax: 905-522-7839; 888-311-4987
E-mail: info@bcdecker.com
www.bcdecker.com

Canada
BC Decker Inc
20 Hughson Street South
P.O. Box 620, LCD 1
Hamilton, Ontario L8N 3K7
Tel: 905-522-7017; 800-568-7281
Fax: 905-522-7839; 888-311-4987
E-mail: info@bcdecker.com
www.bcdecker.com

Foreign Rights
John Scott & Company
International Publishers' Agency
P.O. Box 878
Kimberton, PA 19442
Tel: 610-827-1640
Fax: 610-827-1671
E-mail: jsco@voicenet.com

Japan
Igaku-Shoin Ltd.
Foreign Publications Department
3-24-17 Hongo
Bunkyo-ku, Tokyo, Japan 113-8719
Tel: 3 3817 5680
Fax: 3 3815 6776
E-mail: fd@igaku-shoin.co.jp

U.K., Europe, Scandinavia, Middle East
Elsevier Science
Customer Service Department
Foots Cray High Street
Sidcup, Kent
DA14 5HP, UK
Tel: 44 (0) 208 308 5760
Fax: 44 (0) 181 308 5702
E-mail: cservice@harcourt.com

*Singapore, Malaysia,Thailand, Philippines,
Indonesia, Vietnam, Pacific Rim, Korea*
Elsevier Science Asia
583 Orchard Road
#09/01, Forum
Singapore 238884
Tel: 65-737-3593
Fax: 65-753-2145

Australia, New Zealand
Elsevier Science Australia
Customer Service Department
STM Division, Locked Bag 16
St. Peters, New South Wales, 2044
Australia
Tel: 61 02 9517-8999
Fax: 61 02 9517-2249
E-mail: stmp@harcourt.com.au
www.harcourt.com.au

Mexico and Central America
ETM SA de CV
Calle de Tula 59
Colonia Condesa
06140 Mexico DF, Mexico
Tel: 52-5-5553-6657
Fax: 52-5-5211-8468
E-mail: editoresdetextosmex@prodigy.net.mx

Argentina
CLM (Cuspide Libros Medicos)
Av. Córdoba 2067 - (1120)
Buenos Aires, Argentina
Tel: (5411) 4961-0042/(5411) 4964-0848
Fax: (5411) 4963-7988
E-mail: clm@cuspide.com

Brazil
Tecmedd
Av. Maurílio Biagi, 2850
City Ribeirão Preto – SP – CEP: 14021-000
Tel: 0800 992236
Fax: (16) 3993-9000
E-mail: tecmedd@tecmedd.com.br

Introduction

As travel abroad continues to become cheaper and more accessible to an ever-increasing number of people, it is important that the health risks associated with visiting other countries are seriously addressed.

Many people are unaware of the health risks involved in travelling unprotected to disease risk areas. The *Atlas of Travel Medicine and Health* has been developed to help you improve this situation.

This book should be used as a guide by the healthcare professional when discussing travel health. It is assumed that a complete risk assessment will have been carried out for the traveller before the *Atlas* is referred to. As a result, such information has not been included within this publication.

The *Atlas of Travel Medicine and Health* is intended to be used as a reference tool in conjunction with a number of other reference sources. These include the following:

- Health Information for Overseas Travel, HMSO 2001 edition (£8.50 – ISBN 0 11 322329 3) View online at: https://www.archive.official-documents.co.uk/document/doh/hinfo/travel02.htm

- Guidelines for malaria prevention in travellers from the United Kingdom for 2001. Bradley DJ, Bannister B, on behalf of the Advisory Committee on Malaria Prevention for the UK traveller. *Commun Dis Public Health* 2001;4:84-101. Available to download from the Internet at http://www.phls.org.uk/topics_az/malaria/menu.htm

- Immunisation against Infectious Disease HMSO 1996 edition (£6.95 - ISBN 0 11 321815 X) (Known as the 'green book'). While parts of this book are slightly outdated, this remains, in general, a very valuable publication. Further information can be obtained at http://www.doh.gov.uk

- TRAVAX online database service, Scottish Centre for Infection and Environmental Health, Glasgow (http://www.travax.scot.nhs.uk). Membership is for healthcare professionals only—for further details contact Amanda Burridge, tel 0141 300 1132, or register online. The public site of this service, valuable for travellers, is http://www.fitfortravel.scot.nhs.uk

- International Travel and Health – Vaccination requirements and health advice, World Health Organisation 2002 edition. This book can also be viewed and downloaded from the WHO Website (http://www.who.int/ith/)

Acknowledgment

The authors wish to thank Fernando Boero, for his significant contribution and original work on the malaria maps. Thanks also go to Tomorrow's Guides Ltd., Hungerford, for their permission to use weather statistics from "Weather to Travel" The Travellers' Guide to the World's Weather.

How to Use This Atlas: A Guide for the Healthcare Professional

The atlas is divided into three main sections.

Sections one and two contain information for the healthcare professional only. As outlined on the contents page, these sections include key disease information and general advice about food, water, and personal hygiene; biting insects and bugs; sun and heat; casual sex and blood-borne modes of infection; animal bites, parasitic infection, and other hazards; medical cover/insurance, and accidents. The disease pages contain information on 13 travel-related diseases considered to be among the most important. The information on these pages is for your reference only and is not intended to be shown to the traveller. You may wish, however, to use the endemicity maps for the particular disease if you think this is appropriate in the educational process.

Section three consists of the main part of the atlas. It is intended for use by both the healthcare professional and the traveller, and it contains country-specific information for the top travel destinations, arranged in alphabetical order.

The information provided on each page is as follows:
- A map of the country showing the capital city and, for some countries, an indication of the malaria risk areas
- Vaccination advice (although this should always be used in conjunction with the most up-to-date references)
- Graphs depicting the average daily sunshine, rainfall, and temperature
- Other health considerations

- For further information on any countries not available in this book, details can be found at www.travax.scot.nhs.uk (membership-only site) or, alternatively, on the public site of this service, valuable for travelers, at www.fitfortravel.scot.nhs.uk

Disclaimer

The material contained within the atlas, including endemicity maps, is designed to be used as a guide only. Country-specific information has been taken from a wide range of sources and may vary according to region. Similarly, the information provided on the average daily sunshine, rainfall, and temperature will vary according to region.

While every effort has been made to ensure the accuracy of the information herein supplied, the authors and SCIEH make no warranty, express or implied, as to the accuracy, completeness, or usefulness of the information, and all liability is excluded, save in respect of any personal injury, caused by their negligence.

How to Use the Malaria Maps

Each Country within the *Atlas of Travel Medicine and Health* has a map. For the countries that have a risk of malaria, the malarious areas are shaded in red. There are two levels of risk.

1. Limited malarial risk is shaded in light red.
2. Substantial malarial risk is shaded in darker red.

Areas without a malarial risk are done in various other colours, which have no specific meaning.

These maps are intended only as helpful guides when you are determining whether your traveller is entering a malarious area. Remember that mosquitoes that spread malaria do not always respect boundaries, so while every effort has been taken to ensure that information on the maps is correct, they may not be exact. In addition, seasonal variation in malarial risk is not shown. It is essential that a full risk assessment is carried out, and healthcare professionals should use another up-to-date reference source to help ascertain their patients' risk and whether they should take antimalarial chemoprophylaxis.

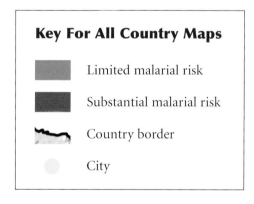

CONTENTS

SECTION 1

SECTION 2

SECTION 3

Country-specific immunisation advice, malaria advice and precautions, and other health topics (includes a map and weather chart for each country)

SECTION 1

Water, Food, and Personal Hygiene: General Advice

- Unless you are sure of the purity of the local water, do not drink it without boiling or sterilizing it first, and avoid ice cubes. If you are unsure, use bottled water in sealed containers: this includes water for cleaning your teeth.
- Unpasteurized milk should be boiled before use. Caution should be exercised with local dairy products including ice cream.
- Remember that all meats should be cooked thoroughly and eaten hot whenever possible.
- Avoid leftovers and reheated food.
- Shellfish is a high-risk food, especially when eaten raw: take local advice, but when in doubt, avoid altogether.
- Eat only cooked vegetables, and avoid salads.
- Peel all fruit.
- As a general rule, avoid purchasing food from roadside food stalls.
- Always wash your hands thoroughly before eating and handling food and after using the toilet.

Accidents

Swimming and road traffic accidents are common among travellers. Most accidents are preventable. Precautions to take include the following:

- Avoid alcohol and food before swimming.
- Do not go swimming alone. Always supervise children.
- Check the depth of the water before diving.
- Never drink and drive.
- If renting a vehicle, choose a large sturdy one that has been well maintained, wherever possible. Avoid travelling at night.
- Whether you are a driver or a pedestrian, always check on local traffic regulations.
- Always wear a helmet on a motorbike, moped, or bicycle.
- Always wear a seat belt in a car.
- If you are going to take part in potentially hazardous sports, such as skiing, canoeing, white water rafting, or paragliding, follow all the relevant safety advice.
- Know the local emergency facilities.
- Travellers to developing countries may wish to carry a sterile medical pack with them—for further details, see "General Advice on Casual Sex and Blood-Borne Modes of Infection."

Animal Bites, Parasitic Infection, and Other Hazards: General Advice

RABIES

Rabies is present worldwide, except in the United Kingdom, parts of Scandinavia, Japan, Oceania, Antarctica, New Zealand, Malta, and some Caribbean islands. The most common route of transmission to humans is via the bite of an infected domestic dog, although other animals also carry the virus. Once the illness has started, rabies will cause death; therefore, prevention of exposure, or postexposure prophylaxis in the event of a bite, is especially important. The following precautions should be taken:

- Do not stroke dogs and cats, and avoid contact with all wild animals.
- In rabies-endemic areas, all unprovoked bites or licks should be considered as possible exposure. In that event, immediate first aid should be administered.
  1. The wound should be cleansed with soap and placed under running water for 5 minutes.
  2. Antiseptic should be applied such as povidone-iodine, or, if not available, 40 to 70% alcohol will do (for example, gin or whisky).
  3. Medical assistance should be sought as soon as possible.
  4. In the event of possible exposure, the owner of the animal should try to be identified and the animal observed for 10 days to see if it begins to behave abnormally. The assistance of local officials may be necessary. If the animal is wild or stray, immediate attempts should be made to identify, capture, or even kill the animal involved to determine whether it is rabid.
- Rabies vaccine should be considered by those who may be exposed to an unusual risk of infection (eg, as a result of their work) or those travelling to remote areas where medical treatment may not be immediately available. Even if immunized, medical treatment is still urgently required following possible rabies exposure.

FRESH WATER PARASITES

Swimming and paddling should be avoided in schistosomiasis-(Bilharzia infection) endemic areas—for further information, see "Schistosomiasis (Bilharzia infection)".

OTHER HAZARDS

More adventurous travellers may be exposed to greater risks (eg, snake bites, scorpion stings, spider bites, marine animals, etc). Further information is available in "Health Information for Overseas Travell"—see references on page 15 or <http://www.archive.official-documents.co.uk/document/doh/hinfo/travel02.htm> (accessed June 3, 2002).

Biting Insects and Bugs: General Advice

In tropical areas, many different mosquitoes, flies, fleas, ticks, and bugs can bite, transmitting a variety of diseases. Many of these arthropods bite at night but some do so during the day. Measures can be taken to prevent these bites.

- Use insect repellent on exposed skin—preferably one containing diethyltoluamide (DEET) or a eucalyptus oil base.
- Wear socks, long trousers, and long-sleeved clothing after sunset. Clothes can be sprayed with repellent or insecticide to give added protection.
- Air conditioning deters the entry of mosquitoes.
- If the sleeping area is screened, ensure windows and screens are closed before dusk. Vapourizing mats and knockdown sprays can be used to kill any mosquitoes that have entered the room during the day. An increased number of devices should be considered in larger rooms.
- If the room is not air conditioned or screened, sleep under a mosquito net, preferably one that is impregnated with an insecticide (for example, permethrin).
- There is no scientific evidence to support the use of garlic, vitamin B, and electric buzzers. They are ineffective.
- Travellers to areas where there is a risk of tick-borne encephalitis should wear long-sleeved clothing and boots with trousers tucked into their socks and use insect repellent if walking in dense undergrowth in forested areas. Self-inspection at the end of each day, to permit prompt removal of attached ticks, is essential.

Sun and Heat: General Advice

Sunburn and heat exhaustion can cause great distress to travellers. Sunburn can produce long-term effects, including skin cancer.

Both conditions are preventable. Precautions to take include:

- Increase exposure to the sun gradually, not more than 20 minutes at a time initially.
- Use protective creams as appropriate and always reapply after washing or swimming.
- Wear sensible protective clothing, including hats, and wear sunglasses to filter ultraviolet (UV) rays.
- Avoid the sun between 11 am and 3 pm when its rays are particularly strong. Remember that you can burn even when swimming, snorkelling, at high altitudes, in the snow or at sea.
- People with pale skin and/or red hair should take special care in the sun.
- Protect infants and children at all times.
- Overexposure to sun in a hot and humid climate can lead to heat exhaustion. Avoid strenuous activity during the hottest hours and make sure that you drink plenty of nonalcoholic liquids to balance the loss of body fluids through perspiration. Be aware that alcohol consumption can make you dehydrated.

General Advice on Casual Sex and Blood-Borne Modes of Infection

If the traveller indulges in casual sex, the risk of infection with a sexually transmitted disease is high. Gonorrhoea and syphilis may cause long-term disability, especially if treatment is delayed. Hepatitis B and the human immuno-deficiency virus (HIV), the cause of acquired immunodeficiency syndrome (AIDS), also are spread sexually as well as by blood transfusion, medical procedures with nonsterile equipment, and sharing of needles (eg, tattooing, body piercing, acupuncture, and intravenous [IV] drug use). Hepatitis C is also transmitted via these routes, especially by IV drug use and transfussion of unscreened blood. The following precautions should be taken:

- Because casual sexual intercourse is risky, condoms should be used. They provide good protection, but not complete protection. (If using condoms, for reliability take products with you displaying the British Kite Mark.) Be aware that hot climates and substances such as suntan oils may degrade rubber.
- Illicit drug use should be avoided as this might put the traveller in contact with people who are HIV positive. The sharing of needles is very dangerous.
- Unless you are absolutely certain that the equipment being used is sterile, skin-damaging procedures such as ear/body piercing, tattooing, and acupuncture should be avoided.
- In many developing countries, re-use of medical supplies, including needles and syringes, is common. Travel packs containing sterile equipment for use in an emergency are available from some pharmacies and travel clinics. A kit should be supplied with a certificate showing the contents and the reason for its purchase. This documentation is useful for clearance at customs.

BLOOD TRANSFUSION

In western Europe, North America, Japan, and Australasia, all donated blood is now screened for HIV antibodies. However, in most developing countries, there may be only the most basic blood transfusion services, and much of the blood donated is unscreened. The risks from blood transfusion in such circumstances are high. Therefore, points to consider are:

- Accidents are the commonest reason for needing a blood transfusion—see "Accidents" for general advice on accident prevention.
- Blood transfusion should only be accepted when essential.
- Pregnancy or any other medical condition that may lead to heavy blood loss should be taken into account before travelling to destinations where good medical facilities will not be available.
- Knowing your blood group in advance may make it easier to find a donor in an emergency.

A charitable organization in the United Kingdom called The Blood Care Foundation operates a Blood Care Programme, that is designed to provide screened blood, in an emergency, to its members in any part of the world. The program is also designed to alleviate the shortages of blood that occur in many parts of the developing world. Further information is available from <http://www.bloodcare.org.uk> (accessed June 3, 2002).

MEDICAL COVER/INSURANCE

- Travel insurance covering both injuries and illness when travelling abroad is essential. A third of all travel insurance claims relate to medical problems.
- Travellers should be encouraged to buy adequate travel insurance to provide comprehensive coverage for cancellation and curtailment, the risks of the trip, and include adequate funds for medical repatriation. The insurance should also include a 24-hour assistance service and, ideally, coverage for legal services.
- Some credit and charge cards provide health insurance for travellers, but this may not provide full travel coverage. The policy must be checked to ensure it is adequate.
- When buying insurance, any medical conditions MUST be declared. It may be necessary to search around for an insurance company to provide adequate protection; some companies may charge a premium for this coverage.
- Travellers going on adventure holidays and "gap year" type travellers may find travel insurance from a specialist company more favourable.
- The group of travellers "visiting friends and relations" (VFRs) should be reminded that travel insurance is an important aspect of their travel arrangements.
- The United Kingdom has mutual health care agreements with countries within the European Economic Area (EEA). However, this only provides free or reduced-cost emergency medical coverage, does not cover all expenses incurred, and never covers provision for the cost of bringing a person back to the United Kingdom in the event of illness or death. This medical coverage is obtained on an E111 form obtainable from the Post Office. The E111 entitles you to the same medical treatment a citizen of that country would receive, but the standard of medical services may not be up to that which we expect from our National Health Service. Countries covered by the form E111 are Austria, Belgium, Denmark, Finland, France, Germany, Greece, Italy, Luxembourg, the Netherlands, Portugal, Spain, Ireland, and Sweden. Besides the countries covered by the E111 form, the United Kingdom has a "reciprocal agreement" with some other countries, most notably Australia, Barbados, Czech Republic, New Zealand, and Russia. The agreement gives travellers the right to the same medical treatment that citizens of these countries receive.

Reference

1. Which Report, April 2001. http://sub.which.net/holiday/reports/apr2001ho22t24/printreport.html (accessed June 6, 2002)

SECTION 2

Malaria

- Malaria is a common and serious tropical disease. It is caused by a protozoan of the genus *Plasmodium* and is transmitted to humans by the bite of an infected female *Anopheles* mosquito, usually between dusk and dawn. Four different species of *Plasmodium* can give rise to human malaria: *P. falciparum, P. vivax, P. ovale,* and *P. malariae,* and of these, *P. falciparum* is the most serious, and is responsible for most of the deaths that occur. Prevention and treatment of *P. falciparum* malaria has become increasingly difficult because its resistance to antimalarial drugs has increased and become more widespread.
- Globally, between 200 and 300 million people are affected by the disease each year and around one million infants and children die from malaria in Africa alone.[1]
- In the year 2000, 2,069 cases of malaria were reported in the United Kindom, including 16 deaths, some of which could have been prevented.[2]
- There are four principles of malaria prevention that should receive attention from both travellers and their advisers and that are essential to prevent suffering due to malaria.[3]

  1. **Awareness: know about the risks.** This entails the traveller needing to know whether malaria is transmitted in the country and area that they are visiting; whether or not chloroquine- or other drug-resistant malaria is present; and the transmission season and the level of transmission.
  2. **Bites by mosquitoes: prevent or avoid.** This will have a significant impact on malaria transmission. This entails ensuring that the traveller is aware that bite prevention is as important as taking chemoprophylaxis. Refer to Chapter 4 for advice on bite prevention.
  3. **Compliance with appropriate chemoprophylaxis.** This entails choosing the appropriate drug suitable for the traveller's destination and their health assessment; ensuring compliance with the medication—the chosen chemoprophylaxis must be taken at the appropriate time interval prior to entering the malarious area, all the time there, and for the correct time after leaving the malarious area; and depending on the choice of chemoprophylaxis selected, ensuring that administration of the chosen chemoprophylaxis is correct. The traveller must be made aware that no chemoprophylaxis is 100% effective.
  4. **Diagnose breakthrough malaria swiftly and obtain treatment promptly.** It is impossible to distinguish early *P. falciparum* malaria from influenza on clinical grounds. Travellers visiting malarious areas need to be aware of the need to seek medical advice promptly for any febrile or flu-like illness occurring within 1 year and especially within 3 months of returning from an endemic area.

References

1. World Health Organization. Roll Back Malaria. http://www.who.int/inf-fs/en/fact203.html (accessed June 6, 2002).
2. New guidance for the prevention of malaria in travellers from the United Kingdom. Commun Dis Rep CDR Wkly 2001;11:3–4.
3. Bradley DJ, Bannister B, on behalf of the Advisory Committee on Malaria Prevention for UK Traveller. Guidelines for malaria prevention in travellers from the United Kingdom for 2001. Commun Dis Public Health 2001;4:84–101. (Accessible at http://www.phls.org.uk/topics_az/malaria/menu.htm.

HOW TO USE THE MALARIA RISK AREA MAPS WITHIN THIS ATLAS

Specific information about appropriate malaria chemoprophylaxis has not been included within this atlas. This information should be obtained from other reference sources as described in the introduction. Advisers may also find the *Guidelines for malaria prevention in travellers from the United Kingdom for 2001* extremely useful to read (see reference 3 on page 9).

Maps of countries where malaria is endemic are shown in the "Country-Specific Information on Malaria, Vaccines, and Other Health Considerations" in Section 3 for the following countries:

Argentina
Armenia
Azerbaijan
Bangladesh
Bolivia
Botswana
Brazil
Cambodia
Cameroon
Central African Republic
China (including Taiwan)
Colombia
Costa Rica
Democratic Republic of Congo
Dominican Republic
Ecuador (including the Galapagos Islands)
Egypt
Ethiopia
Gambia
Ghana
Guatemala
Guyana
Haiti
Hong Kong Sar
India
Indonesia (including Bali)
Iran
Iraq
Kenya
Korea, Democratic Peoples Republic (North Korea)
Korea, Republic of (South Korea)
Lao People's Democratic Republic

Malawi
Malaysia
Mauritius
Mexico
Morocco
Mozambique
Myanmar (formerly Burma)
Namibia
Nepal
Nigeria
Oman
Pakistan
Panama
Papua New Guinea
Peru
Philippines
Saudi Arabia
South Africa
Sri Lanka
Tajikistan
Thailand
Turkey
Turkmenistan
Uganda
United Arab Emirates
United Republic of Tanzania
Venezuela (including Margarita Island)
Vietnam
Yemen
Zambia
Zimbabwe

Global Distribution of Hepatitis A

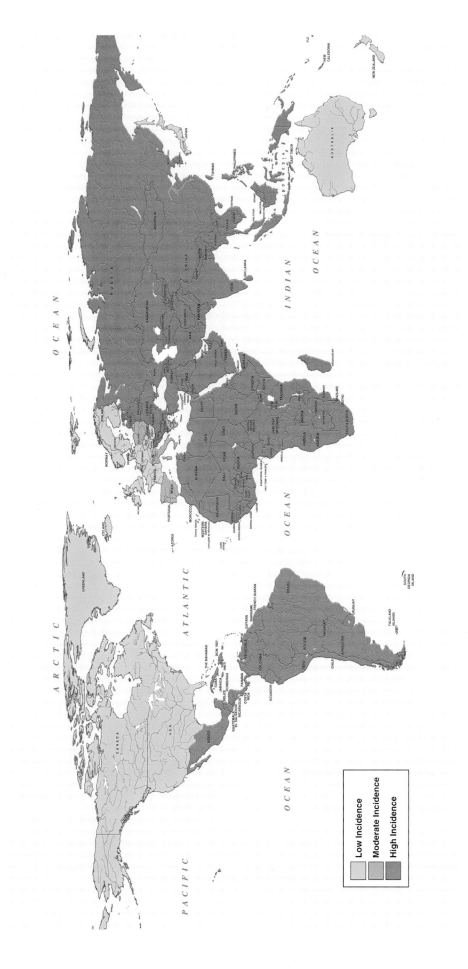

Low Incidence
Moderate Incidence
High Incidence

Source: TRAVAX, Glasgow, Scotland, 2002

12

Hepatitis A

- Hepatitis A is a highly infectious disease caused by a virus (formerly called infectious hepatitis).
- Hepatitis A is transmitted by the faecal-oral route. Person-to-person spread is the most common method of transmission, although contaminated food and drink is a risk to travellers.
- Symptoms include fever, myalgia, and lassitude. Nausea and vomiting are common, followed later by dark urine, pale stools, and jaundice.
- Asymptomatic disease is common in children, and hepatitis A is rarely fatal. However, severity tends to increase with age, with those infected being unable to work for several weeks or months.
- Hepatitis A is the most common vaccine-preventable infection of travellers.[1]
- Hepatitis A is endemic throughout the world and hyperendemic in areas of poor sanitation. Anyone travelling outside northern and western Europe, Scandinavia, North America, Japan, Australia, and New Zealand, should consider being immunized against hepatitis A.
- Immunisation with an inactivated vaccine offers prolonged protection (10 years after a full course).
- Travellers should still adhere to food, water, and personal hygiene advice.
- Travellers should be made aware that shellfish are a common source of hepatitis A (they are filter feeders and concentrate the virus from faecally contaminated water).
- Travellers who have suffered hepatitis A infection will have developed lifelong immunity and will not require vaccination. (This should be confirmed with a blood test.)

Reference

1. Centers for Disease Control and Prevention. Health information for the international traveller 2001–2002. Atlanta: US Department of Health and Human Services, Public Health Service; 2001.

Global Distribution of Chronic Hepatitis B Infection

Source: Centre for Disease Control, Atlanta, GA, 2001

Hepatitis B

- Hepatitis B is an acute viral infection of the liver. Transmission is blood borne, via sexual intercourse, needle sharing, blood transfusion, injections, and other invasive procedures (including tattooing, body piercing, and acupuncture) using inadequately sterilized equipment.
- Symptoms are similar to hepatitis A, although some cases can progress to acute hepatic necrosis. Among cases requiring hospital admission, the fatality rate is about 1%.[1]
- Up to 10% of those infected as adults become chronic carriers of the hepatitis B virus.
- Of those who are hepatitis B carriers, approximately 25% worldwide develop liver disease, leading to cirrhosis in some patients. These patients are also at increased risk of developing hepatocellular carcinoma.[1]
- Hepatitis B is highly endemic in Africa, much of South America, Eastern Europe, the eastern Mediterranean area and SE Asia, China, and the Pacific Islands except Australia, New Zealand, and Japan. In most of these areas, 5 to 15% of the population are chronically infected carriers of the hepatitis B virus.[1]
- Immunisation is recommended in individuals who are at increased risk of hepatitis B because of their lifestyle, occupation, or other factors, such as close contact with a case or carrier.
- Hepatitis B vaccination offers up to 5 years' protection.
- It is important that immunisation against hepatitis B does not encourage relaxation of good infection-control procedures.

Reference

1. World Health Organization. International travel and health—vaccination requirements and health advice. Geneva: WHO; 2001.

Global Distribution of Typhoid

Low Incidence
Moderate Incidence
High Incidence

Source: TRAVAX, Glasgow, Scotland, 2002

Typhoid

- Typhoid fever is a systemic infection caused by the gram-negative bacillus *Salmonella typhi*. (Do not confuse it with *Salmonella typhimurium*.)
- Typhoid fever is spread by the faecal-oral route, usually through food or drink that has been contaminated with the excreta of a human case or carrier.
- Symptoms of this septicaemic illness include fever, headache, abdominal discomfort, constipation, often a dry cough, and sometimes confusion. After 7 to 10 days, the fever reaches a peak, rose spots may appear, and diarrhoea begins.
- Treatment is with antibiotics. If untreated, complications can develop, the most common being intestinal bleeding or perforation, which can cause severe illness and death.
- Typhoid is predominantly a disease of countries with poor sanitation and poor standards of personal and food hygiene, especially in Africa, Asia, Central and South America, and southeast Europe.
- An estimated 16 million cases of typhoid fever and 600,000 related deaths occur worldwide every year.[1]
- Vaccination is available against typhoid in injectable and oral forms, but it must be remembered that the vaccines are not 100% effective.
- Travellers should still adhere to food, water, and personal hygiene advice.

Reference

1. Centers for Disease Control and Prevention. Health information for the international traveller 2001–2002. Atlanta: US Department of Health and Human Services, Public Health Service; 2001.

Yellow Fever Endemic Zones

Yellow Fever Endemic Zone

Source: WHO, Geneva, Switzerland, 2002

Yellow Fever

- Yellow fever is an acute flavivirus infection that is spread by the bite of an infected mosquito. It occurs in tropical areas of Africa and South America.
- Yellow fever ranges in severity from nonspecific symptoms to an illness of sudden onset with fever, vomiting, and prostration, which may progress to haemorrhage and jaundice. At least 50% of the individuals who reach the toxic phase of the disease do not survive.[1]
- Yellow fever vaccine confers immunity in nearly 100% of recipients and immunity persists for at least 10 years.[2]
- The yellow fever vaccine can only be administered at a designated center because an International Certificate of Vaccination is issued after immunisation. This certificate is valid for 10 years from the tenth day after vaccination.
- Yellow fever vaccination is administered for the following reasons:
    1. To protect against yellow fever infection
    2. To allow a yellow fever certificate of vaccination to be given
    3. For both points (1) and (2)
- If yellow fever vaccination is contraindicated, then a certificate of exemption may be provided, but travellers may be at risk of infection if they choose to travel unimmunized.
- There are many additional infections that can be transmitted by mosquitoes; therefore, mosquito bite prevention measures should always be taken.

References

1. World Health Organization. Fact Sheet No. 100: Yellow Fever. http://www.who.int/inf-fs/en/fact100.html (accessed June 3, 2002).
2. Department of Health. Immunisation against infectious disease. London: HMSO; 1996.

Global Distribution of Epidemic Meningococcal Infection

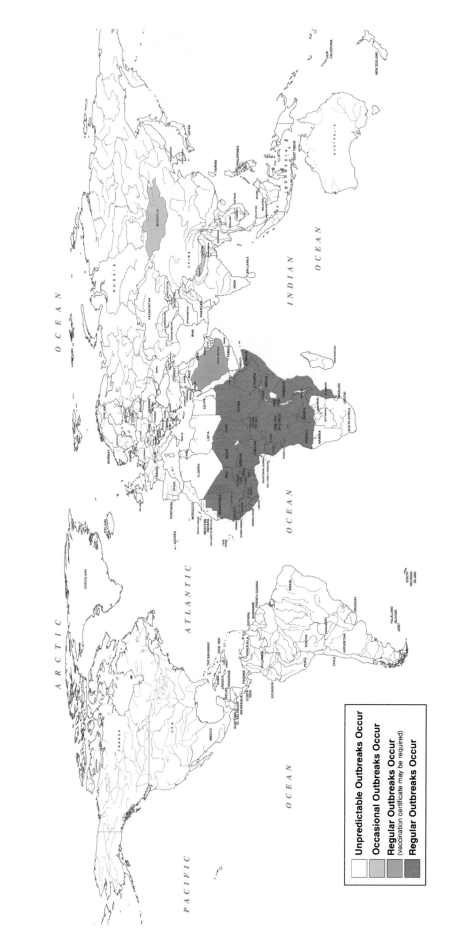

Unpredictable Outbreaks Occur

Occasional Outbreaks Occur

Regular Outbreaks Occur
(vaccination certificate may be required)

Regular Outbreaks Occur

Source: TRAVAX, Glasgow, Scotland, 2002

20

Meningitis

Meningitis is an inflammation of the membranes covering the brain and spinal cord, which is caused by many different types of viruses and bacteria. Bacterial meningitis can be rapidly fatal.

Organisms causing meningitis are transmitted by droplet spread or direct contact from carriers or from individuals in the early stages of the illness; the probable route of invasion is via the nasopharynx.

Meningococcal meningitis is a systemic bacterial infection caused by the organism *Neisseria meningitidis*, which has many pathogenic groups (A,B,C,D,X,Y,Z,W135). Group A organisms cause epidemics, predominantly in sub-Saharan Africa, from Senegal and Gambia in the west to Ethiopia and Somalia in the east and as far south as Zambia, Malawi, and Namibia, particularly in the dry season. Serogroup A and more recently W135, have been responsible for outbreaks in Saudi Arabia in those attending hajj pilgrimages. Group B meningococci remain the prevalent epidemic organisms of Europe and North America, followed by group C.

- Symptoms include fever, malaise, vomiting, headache, photophobia, drowsiness or confusion and joint pains. A typical hemorrhagic rash of meningococcal septicemia may develop. Mortality is 3 to 5% in meningitis and 15 to 20% in septicaemic stages.[1] Prompt treatment is essential.
- Immunisation is presently available only against groups A, C, W135, and Y, which provides 3 to 5 years' protection, depending on the vaccine used.
- Travellers making longer visits (usually 1 month or more to risk areas), especially backpackers and those living or working with local people, are recommended to receive a meningococcal vaccine.
- Travellers attending the hajj annual pilgrimage in Saudi Arabia are required to receive immunisation for A, C, W135, and Y to obtain a visa for entry into the country. A certificate of vaccination should be given to the traveller.
- Meningococcal A and C or quadrivalent vaccine should be advised for all splenectomized travellers visiting any suspected risk area.[2]

References

1. Department of Health. Immunisation against infectious disease. London: HMSO; 1996.
2. UK Departments of Health with the PHLS CDSC. Health information for overseas travel. 2nd ed. London: The Stationery Office; 2001.

Global Distribution of Schistosomiasis

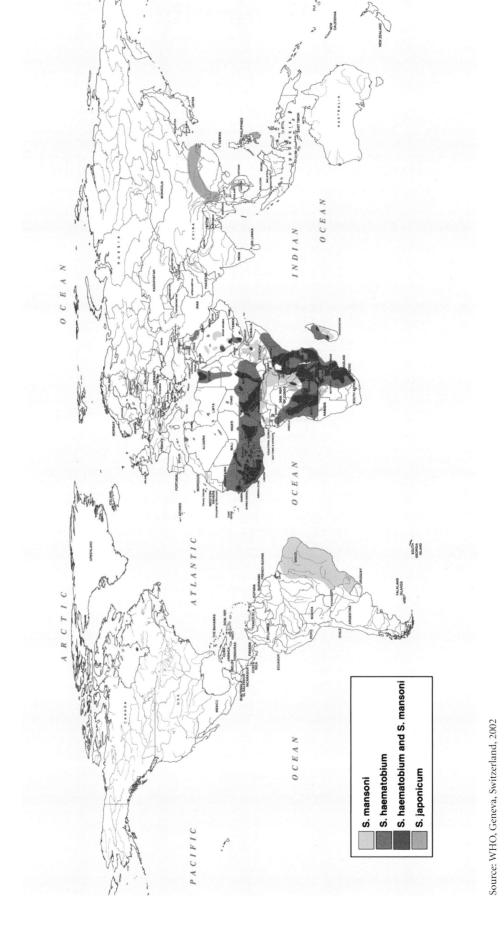

S. mansoni
S. haematobium
S. haematobium and S. mansoni
S. japonicum

Source: WHO, Geneva, Switzerland, 2002

22

Schistosomiasis (Bilharzia infection)

- It is estimated that at least 200 million people around the world are afflicted with schistosomiasis, and it ranks second behind malaria in terms of socioeconomic and public health importance in tropical and subtropical areas.[1]
- Schistosomiasis or Bilharzia infection is infection with a parasitic worm that spends part of its life cycle in fresh water snails and the other part in a human host.
- There are three major species of *Schistosoma*:
    1. *Schistosoma haematobium* found mainly in Africa
    2. *Schistosoma mansoni* found in Africa and eastern South America
    3. *Schistosoma japonicum* found in parts of the Far East
- Schistosomiasis is a far greater problem in Africa than in the Caribbean and Asia.
- The transmission cycle is by the excretion of eggs from the infected human host into a fresh water lake or stream in which certain snails live. The eggs hatch to liberate larvae that infect specific snails. Multiplication of the larvae occurs, and they are released back into the water to penetrate human skin as cercariae. Symptoms may occur when this happens, known as "swimmers' itch." A minimum of 2 to 3 weeks later, a toxaemic illness may occur, called Katayama fever. Whether or not Katayama fever occurs, a chronic phase follows, and once the infection becomes established, abdominal pain and blood in the urine and stool are common.
- Present day diagnosis and treatment can prevent progression of the disease, so that serious problems from chronic disease are rare in travellers.
- There is no available vaccine for this disease.
- Prevention is dependant on avoidance of bathing and paddling in fresh water lakes and streams in an endemic country. Travellers should never assume fresh water to be free from *Schistosoma* in such areas.

Reference

1. World Health Organization. Fact Sheet No. 115. http://www.who.int/inf-fs/en/fact115.html (accessed May 1, 2002).

General Distribution of Dengue 1975–1998

Dengue

Source: WHO, Geneva, Switzerland, 2002

24

Dengue

- Dengue is an arbovirus infection transmitted by the mosquito *Aedes aegypti*.
- After malaria, dengue is the most common and serious mosquito-borne infection affecting travellers.
- Dengue fever is also sometimes called "breakbone fever."
- The disease is endemic in tropical regions, especially in Asia, Africa, Central America, northern parts of South America, and the Carribean, but in recent years has spread and caused major outbreaks in India, Thailand, southern China, Vietnam, Indonesia, the Philippines, and neighbouring countries.[1]
- Symptoms include high fever, headache, and severe joint and muscular pains. A fine maculopapular rash appears around day 4. The illness lasts about 1 week, but full recovery can take far longer.
- There is no vaccine currently available.
- Prevention of the infection is by stringent mosquito bite prevention methods.
- Mosquitoes that transmit dengue, bite mostly during the daytime. Avoid mosquito breeding areas, if known.
- A dangerous variant known as dengue hemorrhagic fever, is particularly prevalent in Southeast Asia. This disease is thought to be related to previous exposure to a different dengue serotype. The illness can develop into uncontrolled bleeding and shock requiring intensive care treatment, and fatality rates can be high.

Reference

1. Halstead SB. Dengue. In: Armstrong D, Cohen J, editors. Infectious diseases. London: Mosby; 1999. p. 6.34.31–34.

Intensity of Wild Poliovirus Transmission in 2000

Certified as Polio Free	
Zero Wild Viruses	
1 to 4 Wild Viruses	
5 to 20 Wild Viruses	
Over 20 Wild Viruses	

Source: WHO, Geneva, Switzerland, 2002

Polio

- Poliomyelitis is an infection caused by one of three types of viruses. The virus first invades the gastrointestinal tract and a viraemic illness may develop. In some cases, the virus invades and destroys the anterior horn cells of the spinal cord. This results in flaccid muscle paralysis, more commonly of the lower limbs. In the most severe cases, the virus attacks the motor neurones of the brain stem causing difficulty in breathing, swallowing, and speaking. In such cases, death can occur unless respiratory support is given.

- Spread is via the faecal-oral route, particularly in areas where there is poor food and water hygiene. Transmission is also possible via droplet infection from the nasopharynx of a person in the acute phase and is more typical in areas where sanitation is good.

- Much of the world has been declared "polio free" and global eradication is anticipated in the future with the World Health Organization setting the year 2005 as the anticipated deadline. However, the disease remains endemic in most of Asia and Africa.[1]

- Currently, travellers to countries not declared polio free should be advised to have up-to-date polio immunisation.

- Prevention of spread can be helped by adopting good food, water, and personal hygiene measures.

- Immunity against polio can be created in two ways: through immunisation and after natural infection with the polio virus. Short-lived natural immunity is acquired through maternal antibodies for 2 or 3 months after birth. Acquiring poliomyelitis will provide lifelong immunity against the disease, but only against the particular type of virus that caused the illness (type 1, 2, or 3). Infection of one type will not provide protection against the other two polio viruses.

- Two different kinds of vaccine are available that will offer immunity against all three types of viruses; oral polio virus as a live vaccine and inactivated polio virus as a killed vaccine, which is useful for administration to those who may be immunosuppressed or pregnant.

- Following live polio vaccination, the traveller should be advised to observe good hand washing measures, to prevent minute quantities of the virus, which may be excreted in the stool, being transmitted to other people for 6 weeks following administration.

Reference

1. World Health Organization. Fact Sheet No 114. http://www.who.int/inf-fs/en/fact114.html (accessed June 3, 2002).

Global Distribution of Japanese B Encephalitis

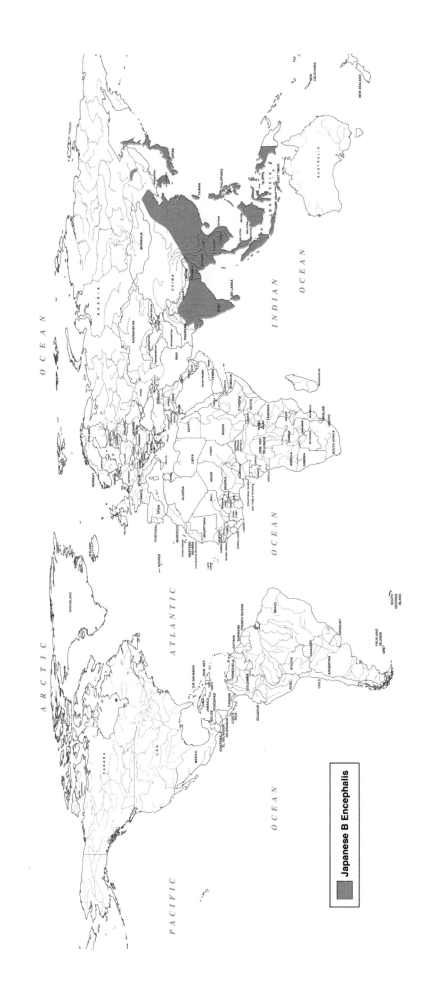

Japanese B Encephalitis

Source: TRAVAX, Glasgow, Scotland, 2002

28

Japanese B Encephalitis

- Japanese encephalitis (JE) is a flavivirus transmitted by various species of culicine mosquito from agricultural animals (often pigs) and birds to humans. These mosquitoes most commonly breed in rice fields.
- The disease exists only in Asia, from India and a small area of Pakistan, eastwards across Thailand and China to Korea and Japan and down through Southeast Asia. It has also recently been reported in the Torres Strait islands between Papua New Guinea and northern Australia.[1]
- The highest risk seasons correlate with the hotter wetter seasons in the northern part of the endemic zone—usually May to October, although in Malaysia, Indonesia, and the Philippines, it tends to be all year round.
- JE infection is asymptomatic in over 99% of cases; however, if the infection develops to a severe encephalitis, there is a 30% mortality rate and about 50% of the survivors are left with neurologic sequelae.[1]
- The disease is extremely rare in travellers, estimated at less than 0.1% in 100,000 tourists and business people.
- Risk is increased for those staying in rural and especially agricultural areas within the endemic zone and in the transmission season.
- Vaccination to offer protection against JE should be considered for those who will be at increased risk for at least 1 month. Possible adverse events, including delayed allergic reactions, indicate that the vaccine course should be completed preferably 14 days before travel. Those with history of urticaria or multiple allergies are considered at higher risk of allergic reactions. Rare neurologic adverse events also occur. Following vaccination, the traveller should be closely observed for 30 minutes in the medical facility.
- Travellers should be advised to maintain adequate bite prevention measures particularly between dusk and dawn to help prevent JE.

Reference

1. UK Departments of Health with the PHLS CDSC. Health information for overseas travel. 2nd ed. London: The Stationery Office; 2001.

Global Distribution of Tick-Borne Encephalitis

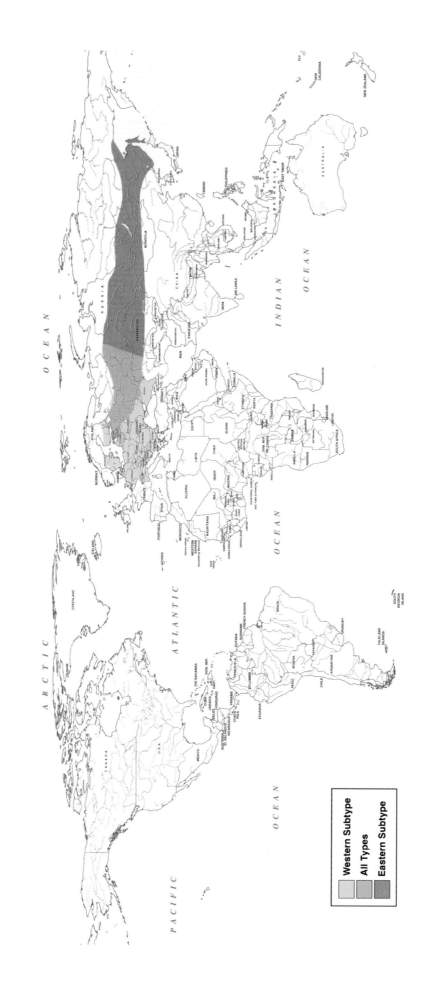

Western Subtype
All Types
Eastern Subtype

Source: TRAVAX, Glasgow, Scotland, 2002

Tick-Borne Encephalitis

- Tick-borne encephalitis (TBE) is a flavivirus transmitted by the vector tick *Ixodes ricinus* and less commonly by the ingestion of unpasteurized milk from infected animals, especially goats.
- TBE exists in Scandinavia, across central and eastern Europe, and the western part of the former USSR. The countries most affected are Austria, Belarus, Croatia, Czech Republic, Estonia, Germany, Hungary, Latvia, Lithuania, Poland, Russia, Slovakia, and the Ukraine. Areas with lower prevalence, or where sporadic cases have been reported, include Albania, Bulgaria, Denmark (Bornholm Island), southwest coast of Finland, France, Greece, Italy, Norway, Romania, Serbia, and the Baltic coast of southern Sweden and Switzerland.[1]
- The infection is asymptomatic in 90% of cases, especially in children. Of those who develop flu-like illness, 10% may suffer a relapse with encephalitis, with possible neurologic sequelae or death. The prognosis is worse with increasing age.
- Risk is mainly to those working, walking, or camping in rural areas where ticks are prevalent, with the greatest incidence from April to August and sometimes October.
- Prevention is by taking precautions against tick bite (see "Biting Insects and Bugs: General Advice"), avoidance of consumption of unpasteurized dairy products, and by vaccination.
- Any ticks that are found should be removed with tweezers as soon as possible, as close to the skin attachment as possible, by pulling steadily but not jerking or twisting. Medical advice should be sought as soon as possible to advise on treatment.
- Inactivated vaccine is available for those considered at risk. Immunisation should ideally be completed 1 month prior to travel. Experience with TBE vaccine in the United Kingdom is limited.

Reference

1. UK Departments of Health with the PHLS CDSC. Health information for overseas travel. 2nd ed. London: The Stationery Office; 2001.

Rabies

- Rabies is a viral disease that infects domestic and wild animals. It is transmitted to other animals and humans through close contact with saliva from infected animals (eg, bites, scratches, and licks on broken skin and mucous membranes.)
- Once symptoms of the disease develop, rabies is fatal to both animals and humans.
- The annual number of deaths worldwide caused by rabies is estimated to be between 40,000 and 70,000. An estimated 10 million people receive postexposure treatments each year after being exposed to suspected rabid animals.[1]
- Whereas the United Kingdom, parts of Scandinavia, Japan, Oceania, Antarctica, New Zealand, Malta, and some Caribbean islands are rabies free, rabies is endemic in most countries in the world.
- The incubation period of rabies is generally between 2 and 8 weeks but may range from 9 days to 2 or more years.
- The first symptoms of rabies are usually nonspecific and suggest involvement of the respiratory, gastrointestinal, and/or central nervous systems. Presentation may include paresthesia around the site of the wound, fever, headache, and malaise. In the acute stage, the disease may present with spasms, hydrophobia, hallucinations, and maniacal behavior progressing to paralysis and coma resulting in death, usually from respiratory failure.
- Rabies vaccine prior to travel is recommended for those who may be exposed to an unusual risk of infection or who are undertaking long journeys in remote areas where medical treatment may not be immediately available.
- Follow general advice for "Animal Bites, Parasitic Infection, and Other Hazards" in Chapter 3 if rabies infection is suspected.
- It is essential to advise travellers to seek immediate medical help for postexposure prophylaxis if infection is suspected. This would consist of rabies vaccine and possibly antirabies immunoglobulin, depending on the extent of the wound and availability of the human rabies immunoglobulin. Postexposure prophylaxis must be administered as soon as possible.

Reference

1. World Health Organizastion. Fact Sheet No 99: Rabies. http://www.who.int/inf-fs/en/fact099.html (accessed June 6, 2002).

Travellers' Diarrhoea

- This is the most common illness that travellers will be exposed to abroad. There is no vaccine yet available to give protection against it, although development of vaccines against some of the causes is underway.
- The illness is very common in those who travel from industrialized to developing countries.[1]
- High risk areas for travellers' diarrhoea include North Africa, sub-Saharan Africa, the Indian subcontinent, Southeast Asia, South America, Mexico, and the Middle East. Medium risk areas include the northern Mediterranean, Canary Islands, and the Caribbean Islands, and low risk areas include North America, western Europe, and Australia.[2]
- Travellers' diarrhoea is caused by ingestion of the causative organisms, which can be bacterial, viral, or parasitic. The most common sources of travellers' diarrhoea are contaminated food and, to a lesser extent, water. Enteropathogens survive in ice and swimming pools. Sea water, heavily contaminated with sewage and faecal microorganisms, is another source.
- Prevention is behavioural—see "Water, Food, and Personal Hygiene: General Advice" in Chapter 1
- Symptoms include four or more loose stools in a 24-hour period, often accompanied by stomach pain, cramps, and vomiting. Travellers' diarrhoea usually lasts 2 to 4 days. It is not life threatening, but if severe dehydration develops, this can be extremely dangerous, especially in young children, the elderly, and those with pre-existing medical problems.
- The mainstay of treatment is rehydration. The use of rehydration solution is extremely useful, especially in severe cases and particularly for children and the elderly. Rehydration solution can be commercially prepared (eg, Dioralyte®, Electrolade®) or home made, in a quantity of 1 teaspoon of sugar and a pinch of salt in a glass (about 250 mL) of freshly boiled water flavoured to taste with fresh orange juice.[3] Adults should drink one glass of solution per hour, plus one glass for every bowel movement, and children should be encouraged to drink as much as possible, until the urine passed is of a normal colour and volume.[3]
- Antimotility drugs can be useful (eg, Imodium® or Lomotil®), but these should never be used in children under 4 years of age and only on prescription for children aged 4 to 12 years. None of these tablets should ever be used if the person has a fever or blood in the stool.
- Medical help should be sought if the affected person has a fever, blood in the diarrhoea, diarrhoea for more than 48 hours (or 24 hours in children), or becomes confused.
- In very special circumstances, antibiotics are sometimes used for chemoprophylaxis, but this must be reviewed by the patient's doctor.
- Remember to inform female travellers taking the oral contraceptive pill that full contraceptive protection may be lost if they suffer diarrhoea and vomiting, and they will need to use extra protection.

References

1. Castelli F, Pezzoli C, Thomasoni L. Epidemiology of travellers' diarrhoea. J Travel Med 2001;8 Suppl 2:S26–30.
2. Cook GC, editor. Manson's tropical diseases. 20th ed. London: WB Saunders Company Ltd; 1996.
3. UK Departments of Health with the PHLS CDSC. Health information for overseas travel. 2nd ed. 2001. London: The Stationery Office; 2001.

SECTION 3

ALBANIA

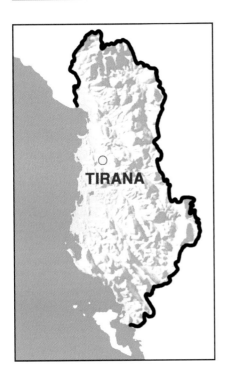

IMMUNISATION ADVICE

- Immunisations recommended in Britain should be up to date, especially those for children and tetanus boosters for adults.
- Coursed or boosters of heptitis A and diphtheria are usually advised.
- Vaccines sometimes recommended are: poliomyelitis, tuberculosis, hepatitis B, tick-borne encephalitis, and typhoid.
- A certificate of vaccination for yellow fever is required for anyone over 1 year of age entering from an infected area.
- Malaria is not normally present.

OTHER HEALTH CONSIDERATIONS

- Water, food, and personal hygiene advice (including prevention of travellers' diarrhoea)
- Insect bite avoidance
- Avoidance of animal bites (to lessen the risk of rabies)
- Sun and heat precautions (in summer months)
- Accident risks (possibility of carrying a sterile medical pack)
- Risks associated with casual sex and prevention of blood-borne infections
- Full medical insurance

WEATHER – Tirana

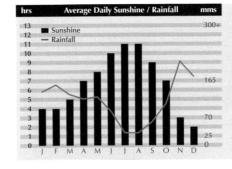

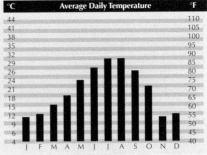

ANTIGUA AND BARBUDA

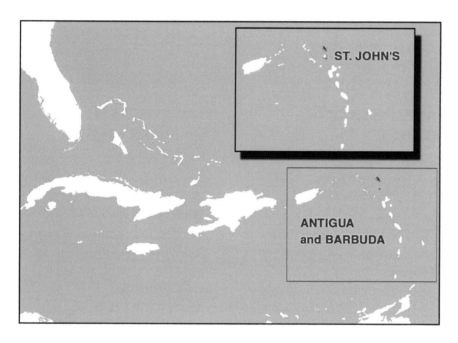

OTHER HEALTH CONSIDERATIONS

- Water, food and personal hygiene advice (including prevention of travellers' diarrhoea)
- Insect bite avoidance (to reduce risk of dengue)
- Avoidance of animal bites
- Sun and heat precautions
- Accident risks
- Risks associated with casual sex and prevention of blood-borne infections
- Full medical insurance

IMMUNISATION ADVICE

- Immunisations recommended in Britain should be up to date, especially those for children and tetanus boosters for adults.
- A course or booster of hepatitis A vaccine is usually advised.
- Vaccines sometimes recommended are: typhoid, diphtheria, tuberculosis, and hepatitis B.
- A certificate of vaccination for yellow fever is required for anyone over 1 year of age and entering from an infected area.
- Malaria is not normally present.

WEATHER – St. John's

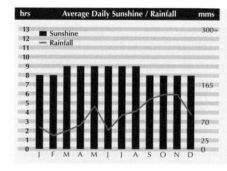

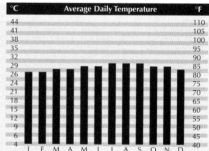

ARGENTINA

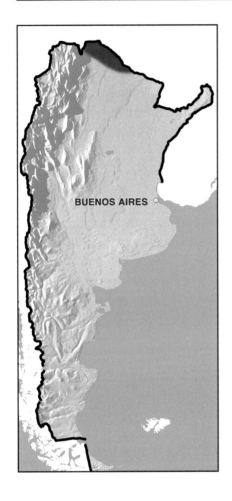

BUENOS AIRES

Malaria Precautions

- Malaria precautions are essential only in the far north west of the country, all year round. Avoid mosquito bites by covering up with clothing (long sleeves and long trousers) especially after sunset, using insect repellents on exposed skin, and, when necessary, sleeping under an impregnated mosquito net.
- Check with your doctor or nurse about suitable antimalarial tablets.
- Prompt investigation of fever is essential.

IMMUNISATION ADVICE

- Immunisations recommended in Britain should be up to date, especially those for children and tetanus boosters for adults.
- A course or booster of hepatitis A is usually advised.

- Vaccines sometimes recommended are: typhoid, diphtheria, hepatitis B, rabies, and tuberculosis.
- No certificate of vaccination for yellow fever is required.

OTHER HEALTH CONSIDERATIONS

- Water, food, and personal hygiene advice (including prevention of travellers' diarrhoea)
- Insect bite avoidance
- Avoidance of animal bites (to lessen the risk of rabies)
- Sun and heat precautions in summer months
- Accident risks (possibility of carrying a sterile medical pack)
- Risks associated with casual sex and prevention of blood-borne infections
- Full medical insurance

MALARIA ADVICE

- Malaria is a serious and sometimes fatal disease transmitted by mosquitoes. There is no vaccine available for malaria.

WEATHER – Buenos Aires

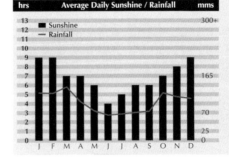

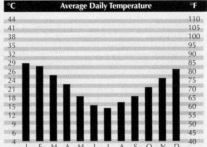

ARMENIA

MALARIA ADVICE

- Malaria is a serious and some-times fatal disease transmitted by mosquitoes. There is no vaccine available for malaria.

Malaria Precautions

- Malaria precautions are essential in some villages in the Ararat Valley, not normally visited by tourists from June to October. Avoid mosquito bites by covering up with clothing (long sleeves and long trousers) especially after sunset, using insect repellants on exposed skin, and, when necessary, sleeping under an impregnated mosquito net.

- Check with your doctor or nurse about suitable antimalarial tablets.
- Prompt investigation of fever is essential.

IMMUNISATION ADVICE

- Immunisations recommended in Britain should be up to date, especially those for children and tetanus boosters for adults.
- Coursed or boosters of heptitis A and diphtheria vaccines are usually advised.
- Vaccines sometimes recom-mended are: diphtheria, tuberculosis, typhoid, rabies, tick-borne encephalitis, poliomyelitis, and hepatitis B.
- No certificate of vaccination for yellow fever is required.

OTHER HEALTH CONSIDERATIONS

- Water, food, and personal hygiene advice (including prevention of travellers' diarrhoea)
- Insect bite avoidance
- Avoidance of animal bites (to lessen the risk of rabies)
- Sun and heat precautions (in summer months)
- Accident risks (possibility of carrying a sterile medical pack)
- Risks associated with casual sex and prevention of blood-borne infections
- Full medical insurance

WEATHER – Yerevan

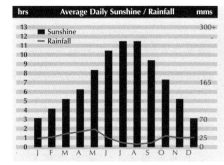

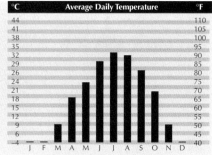

AUSTRALIA

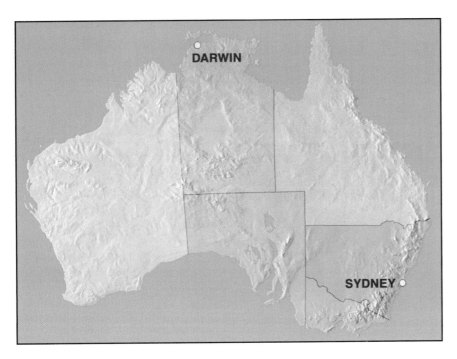

IMMUNISATION ADVICE

- Immunisations recommended in Britain should be up to date, especially those for children.
- A certificate of vaccination for yellow fever is required for anyone over 1 year of age and entering Australia within 6 days of leaving an infected area.
- Malaria is not normally present.

OTHER HEALTH CONSIDERATIONS

- Insect bite avoidance (to reduce risk of dengue)
- Avoidance of animal bites
- Sun and heat precautions
- Accident risks
- Risks associated with casual sex and prevention of blood-borne infections
- Full medical insurance

WEATHER – Sydney and Darwin

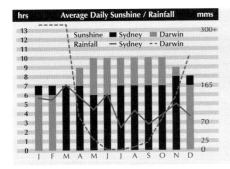

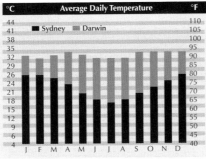

AZERBAIJAN

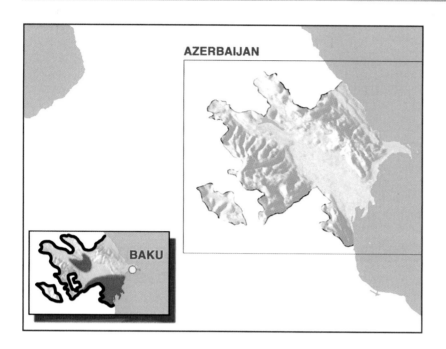

AZERBAIJAN

BAKU

- Courses or boosters of hepatitis A, typhoid, and diphtheria vaccines are usually advised.
- Vaccines sometimes recommended are: tick-borne encephalitis, hepatitis B, poliomyelitis, rabies, and tuberculosis
- No certificate of vaccination for yellow fever is required.

OTHER HEALTH CONSIDERATIONS

- Water, food, and personal hygiene advice (including prevention of travellers' diarrhoea)
- Insect bite avoidance
- Avoidance of animal bites (to lessen the risk of rabies)
- Sun and heat precautions (in summer months)
- Accident risks (possibility of carrying a sterile medical pack)
- Risks associated with casual sex and prevention of blood-borne infections
- Full medical insurance

MALARIA ADVICE

- Malaria is a serious and sometimes fatal disease transmitted by mosquitoes. There is no vaccine available for malaria.

Malaria Precautions

- Malaria precautions are essential only in the southern border regions and the Khackmas region of the north, from June to October. Sporadic cases have been reported in the Baku suburbs. Avoid mosquito bites by covering up with clothing (long sleeves and long trousers) especially after sunset, using insect repellents on exposed skin, and, when necessary, sleeping under an impregnated mosquito net.
- Check with your doctor or nurse about suitable antimalarial tablets.
- Prompt investigation of fever is essential.

IMMUNISATION ADVICE

- Immunisations recommended in Britain should be up to date, especially those for children and tetanus boosters for adults.

WEATHER – Baku

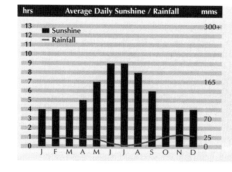

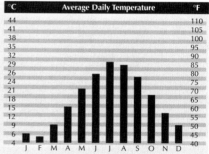

BAHAMAS

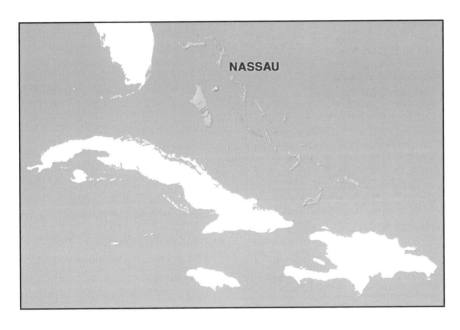

OTHER HEALTH CONSIDERATIONS

- Water, food, and personal hygiene advice (including prevention of travellers' diarrhoea)
- Insect bite avoidance (to reduce risk of dengue)
- Avoidance of animal bites
- Sun and heat precautions
- Accident risks
- Risks associated with casual sex and prevention of blood-borne infections
- Full medical insurance

IMMUNISATION ADVICE

- Immunisations recommended in Britain should be up to date, especially those for children and tetanus boosters for adults.
- A course or booster of hepatitis A vaccine is usually advised.
- Vaccines sometimes recommended are: diphtheria, typhoid, tuberculosis, and hepatitis B.
- A certificate of vaccination for yellow fever is required for anyone over 1 year of age entering from an infected area.
- Malaria is not normally present.

WEATHER – Nassau

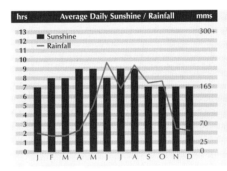

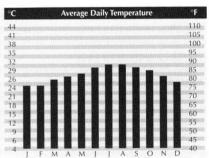

BAHRAIN

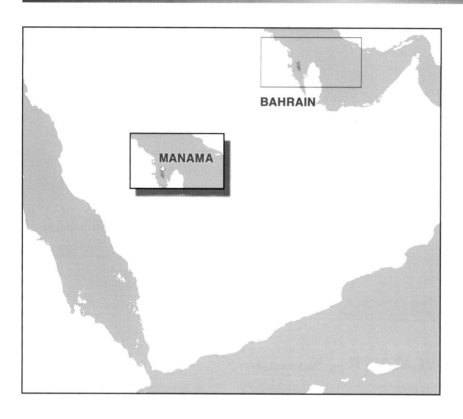

BAHRAIN

MANAMA

OTHER HEALTH CONSIDERATIONS

- Water, food, and personal hygiene advice (including prevention of travellers' diarrhoea)
- Insect bite avoidance (to reduce risk of dengue)
- Avoidance of animal bites (to lessen the risk of rabies)
- Sun and heat precautions
- Accident risks
- Risks associated with casual sex and prevention of blood-borne infections
- Full medical insurance

IMMUNISATION ADVICE

- Immunisations recommended in Britain should be up to date, especially those for children and tetanus boosters for adults.
- A course or booster of hepatitis A vaccine is usually advised.
- Vaccines sometimes recommended are: diphtheria, hepatitis B, rabies, poliomyelitis, tuberculosis, and typhoid.
- No certificate of vaccination for yellow fever is required.
- Malaria is not normally present.

WEATHER – Manama

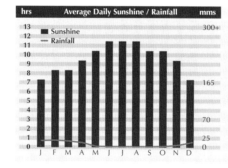

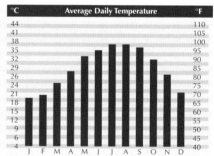

BANGLADESH

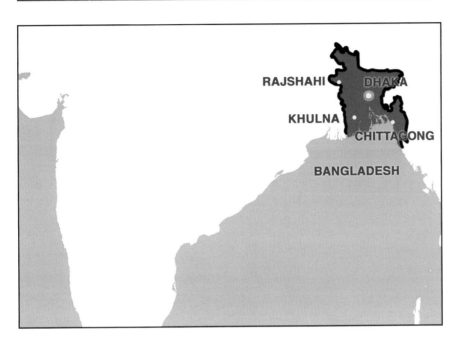

MALARIA ADVICE

- Malaria is a serious and sometimes fatal disease transmitted by mosquitoes. There is no vaccine available for malaria.

Malaria Precautions

- Malaria precautions are essential in all areas, except Dhaka City, all year round. Avoid mosquito bites by covering up with clothing (long sleeves and long trousers) especially after sunset, using insect repellents on exposed skin, and, when necessary, sleeping under an impregnated mosquito net.
- Check with your doctor or nurse about suitable antimalarial tablets.
- Prompt investigation of fever is essential. A person travelling to remote areas should carry, for emergency, standby treatment.

IMMUNISATION ADVICE

- Immunisations recommended in Britain should be up to date, especially those for children and poliomyelitis and tetanus boosters for adults.
- Courses or boosters of diphtheria hepatitis A and typhoid are usually advised.

- Vaccines sometimes recommended are: hepatitis B, rabies, tuberculosis, and Japanese B encephalitis.
- A certificate of vaccination for yellow fever is required if entering Bangladesh within 6 days of passing through or leaving an infected area. Persons without certificates will be detained for 6 days.

OTHER HEALTH CONSIDERATIONS

- Water, food, and personal hygiene advice (including prevention of travellers' diarrhoea)
- Insect bite avoidance (to reduce risk of dengue)
- Avoidance of animal bites (to lessen the risk of rabies)
- Sun and heat precautions
- Accident risks (possibility of carrying a sterile medical pack)
- Risks associated with casual sex and prevention of blood-borne infections
- Full medical insurance

WEATHER – Dhaka

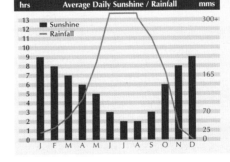

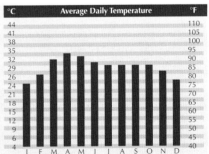

BARBADOS

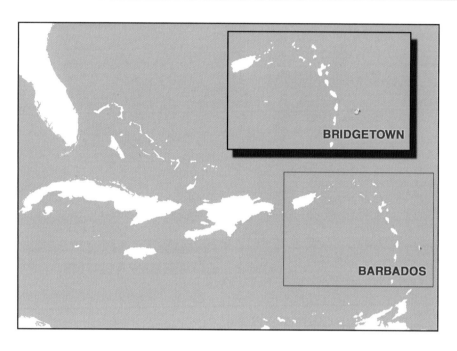

BRIDGETOWN

BARBADOS

OTHER HEALTH CONSIDERATIONS

- Water, food, and personal hygiene advice (including prevention of travellers' diarrhoea)
- Insect bite avoidance (to reduce risk of dengue)
- Avoidance of animal bites
- Sun and heat precautions
- Accident risks
- Risks associated with casual sex and prevention of blood-borne infections
- Full medical insurance

IMMUNISATION ADVICE

- Immunisations recommended in Britain should be up to date, especially those for children and tetanus boosters for adults.
- A course or booster of hepatitis A vaccine is usually advised.
- Vaccines sometimes recommended are: typhoid, diphtheria, hepatitis B, and tuberculosis.
- A certificate of vaccination for yellow fever is required for anyone over 1 year of age entering from an infected area.
- Malaria is not normally present.

WEATHER – Bridgetown

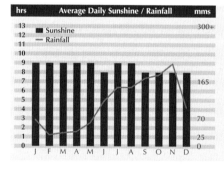

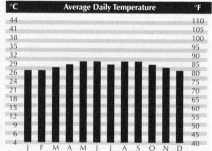

BOLIVIA

MALARIA ADVICE

- Malaria is a serious and sometimes fatal disease transmitted by mosquitoes. There is no vaccine available for malaria.

Malaria Precautions

- Malaria precautions are essential in most areas below 2500 m, all year round. Avoid mosquito bites by covering up with clothing (long trousers) especially after sunset, using insect repellents on exposed skin, and, when necessary, sleeping under an impregnated mosquito net.
- Check with your doctor or nurse about suitable antimalarials.
- Prompt investigation of fever is essential. A person travelling to remote areas should carry, for emergency, standby treatment.

IMMUNISATION ADVICE

- Immunisations recommended in Britain should be up to date, especially those for children and tetanus boosters for adults.
- Courses or boosters of hepatitis A, typhoid, and yellow fever vaccines (east of the Andes and the subtropical part of La Paz department) are usually advised.
- Vaccines sometimes recommended are: hepatitis B, rabies, diphtheria, and tuberculosis.
- A certificate of vaccination for yellow fever is required for anyone entering from an infected area.

OTHER HEALTH CONSIDERATIONS

- Water, food, and personal hygiene advice (including prevention of travellers' diarrhoea)
- Insect bite avoidance (to reduce risk of dengue)
- Avoidance of animal bites (to lessen the risk of rabies)
- Sun and heat precautions
- Accident risks (possibility of carrying a sterile medical pack)
- Risks associated with casual sex and prevention of blood-borne infections
- Full medical insurance

WEATHER – La Paz

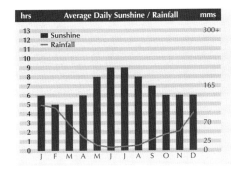

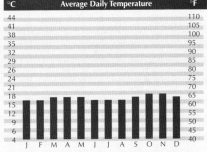

BOSNIA AND HERZEGOVINA

SARAJEVO ○

OTHER HEALTH CONSIDERATIONS

- Water, food, and personal hygiene advice (including prevention of travellers' diarrhoea)
- Insect bite avoidance
- Avoidance of animal bites (to lessen the risk of rabies)
- Sun and heat precautions (in summer months)
- Accident risks (possibility of carrying a sterile medical pack)
- Risks associated with casual sex and prevention of blood-borne infections
- Full medical insurance

IMMUNISATION ADVICE

- Immunisations recommended in Britain should be up to date, especially those for children and tetanus boosters for adults.
- A course or booster of hepatitis A vaccine is usually advised.
- Vaccines sometimes recommended are: poliomyelitis, typhoid, hepatitis B, diphtheria, tuberculosis, tick-borne encephalitis, and rabies.
- No certificate of vaccination for yellow fever is required.
- Malaria is not normally present.

WEATHER – Sarajevo

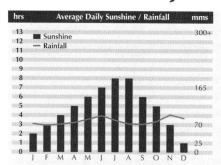

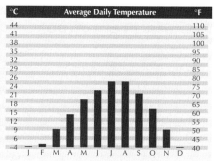

BOTSWANA

MALARIA ADVICE

- Malaria is a serious and some-times fatal disease transmitted by mosquitoes. There is no vaccine available for malaria.

Malaria Precautions

- Malaria precautions are essential in the northern parts of the country (Boteti, Chobe, Ngamiland, Okavano, and Tutume districts) from November to June. Avoid mosquito bites by covering up with clothing (long sleeves and long trousers) especially after sunset, using insect repellents on exposed skin, and, when necessary, sleeping under an impregnated mosquito net.
- Check with your doctor or nurse about suitable antimalarial tablets.

- Prompt investigation of fever is essential. A person travelling to remote areas should carry, for emergency, standby treatment.

IMMUNISATION ADVICE

- Immunisations recommended in Britain should be up to date, especially those for children and tetanus boosters for adults.

- Courses or boosters of hepatitis A and typhoid vaccines are usually advised.
- Vaccines sometimes recommended are: tuberculosis, hepatitis B, rabies, poliomyelitis, and diphtheria.
- No certificate of vaccination for yellow fever required.

OTHER HEALTH CONSIDERATIONS

- Water, food, and personal hygiene advice (including prevention of travellers' diarrhoea)
- Insect bite avoidance
- Avoidance of animal bites (to lessen the risk of rabies)
- Other hazards such as bilharzia
- Sun and heat precautions
- Accident risks (possibility of carrying a sterile medical pack)
- Risks associated with casual sex and prevention of blood-borne infections
- Full medical insurance

WEATHER – Francistown

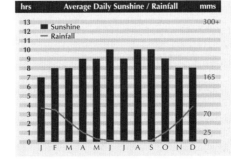

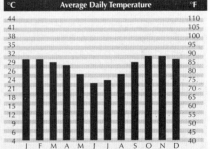

BRAZIL

MALARIA ADVICE

- Malaria is a serious and sometimes fatal disease transmitted by mosquitoes. There is no vaccine available for malaria.

Malaria Precautions

- Malaria precautions are essential in Amazon regions all year round. There is very little risk in Rio de Janeiro and São Paulo. Avoid mosquito bites by covering up with clothing (long sleeves and long trousers) especially after sunset, using insect repellents on exposed skin, and, when necessary, sleeping under an impregnated mosquito net.
- Check with your doctor or nurse about suitable antimalarial tablets.

- Prompt investigation of fever is essential. A person travelling to remote areas should carry, for emergency, standby treatment.

IMMUNISATION ADVICE

- Immunisations recommended in Britain should be up to date, especially those for children and tetanus boosters for adults.

- Courses or boosters of diphtheria, hepatitis A, typhoid and yellow fever (mainly for Western and Amazonian areas) vaccines are usually advised.
- Vaccines sometimes recommended are: hepatitis B, rabies, and tuberculosis.
- A certificate of vaccination for yellow fever is required for anyone over 9 months of age entering from an infected area.

OTHER HEALTH CONSIDERATIONS

- Water, food, and personal hygiene advice (including prevention of travellers' diarrhoea)
- Insect bite avoidance (to reduce risk of dengue)
- Avoidance of animal bites (to lessen the risk of rabies)
- Other hazards such as bilharzia
- Sun and heat precautions
- Accident risks (possibility of carrying a sterile medical pack)
- Risks associated with casual sex and prevention of blood-borne infections
- Full medical insurance

WEATHER – Manaus and Rio de Janeiro

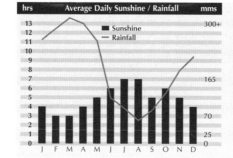

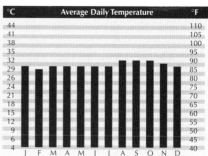

BULGARIA

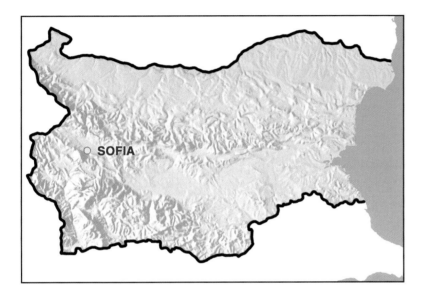

○ SOFIA

OTHER HEALTH CONSIDERATIONS

- Water, food, and personal hygiene advice (including prevention of travellers' diarrhoea)
- Insect bite avoidance
- Avoidance of animal bites (to lessen the risk of rabies)
- Sun and heat precautions
- Accident risks
- Risks associated with casual sex and prevention of blood-borne infections
- Full medical insurance

IMMUNISATION ADVICE

- Immunisations recommended in Britain should be up to date, especially those for children and tetanus boosters for adults.
- A course or booster of hepatitis A vaccine is usually advised.
- Vaccines sometimes recommended are: poliomyelitis, typhoid, tuberculosis, diphtheria, hepatitis B, and tick-borne encephalitis.
- Rabies is present, but postexposure treatment should be readily available.
- No certificate of vaccination for yellow fever is required.
- Malaria is not normally present.

WEATHER – Sofia

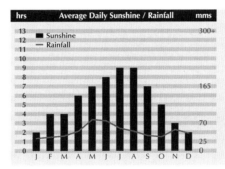

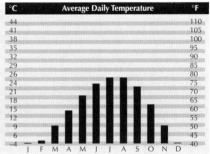

CAMBODIA

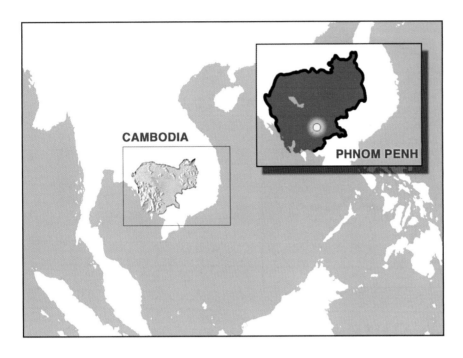

CAMBODIA

PHNOM PENH

MALARIA ADVICE

- Malaria is a serious and some-times fatal disease transmitted by mosquitoes. There is no vaccine available for malaria.

Malaria Precautions

- Malaria precautions are advised in all areas, except Phnom Penh and the river delta, all year round. Avoid mosquito bites by covering up with clothing (long sleeves and long trousers) especially after sunset, using insect repellents on exposed skin, and, when necessary, sleeping under an impregnated mosquito net.
- Check with your doctor or nurse about suitable antimalarial tablets.
- Prompt investigation of fever is essential. A person travelling to remote areas should carry, for emergency, standby treatment.

IMMUNISATION ADVICE

- Immunisations recommended in Britain should be up to date, especially those for children and tetanus boosters for adults.
- Courses or boosters of diphtheria, hepatitis A, and typhoid vaccines are usually advised.

- Vaccines sometimes recom-mended are: Japanese B encephalitis, rabies, tuberculosis, hepatitis B, and poliomyelitis.
- A certificate of vaccination for yellow fever is required if entering from an infected area.

OTHER HEALTH CONSIDERATIONS

- Water, food, and personal hygiene advice (including prevention of travellers' diarrhoea)
- Insect bite avoidance (to reduce risk of dengue)
- Avoidance of animal bites (to lessen the risk of rabies)
- Sun and heat precautions
- Accident risks (possibility of carrying a sterile medical pack)
- Risks associated with casual sex and prevention of blood-borne infections
- Full medical insurance

WEATHER – Phnom Penh

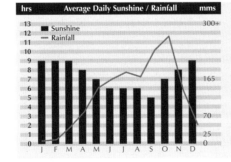
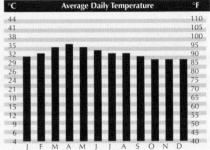

CAMEROON

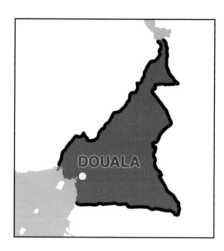

MALARIA ADVICE

- Malaria is a serious and sometimes fatal disease transmitted by mosquitoes. There is no vaccine available for malaria.

Malaria Precautions

- Malaria precautions are essential in all areas, all year round. Avoid mosquito bites by covering up with clothing (long sleeves and long trousers) especially after sunset, using insect repellents on exposed skin, and, when necessary, sleeping under an impregnated mosquito net.
- Check with your doctor or nurse about suitable antimalarial tablets.
- Prompt investigation of fever is essential. A person travelling to remote areas should carry, for emergency, standby treatment.

IMMUNISATION ADVICE

- Immunisations recommended in Britain should be up to date, especially those for children and tetanus boosters for adults.
- Courses or boosters of diphtheria, hepatitis A, typhoid and yellow fever vaccines are usually advised.
- Vaccines sometimes recommended are: meningococcal A and C, poliomyelitis, hepatitis B, rabies, and tuberculosis.
- A certificate of vaccination for yellow fever is mandatory for all travellers over 1 year of age.

OTHER HEALTH CONSIDERATIONS

- Water, food, and personal hygiene advice (including prevention of travellers' diarrhoea)
- Insect bite avoidance (to reduce risk of dengue)
- Avoidance of animal bites (to lessen the risk of rabies)
- Other hazards such as bilharzia
- Sun and heat precautions
- Accident risks (possibility of carrying a sterile medical pack)
- Risks associated with casual sex and prevention of blood-borne infections
- Full medical insurance

WEATHER – Douala

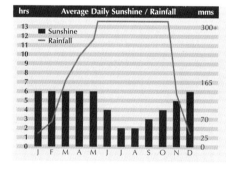

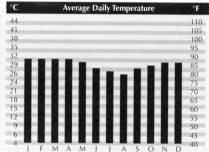

CAYMAN ISLANDS

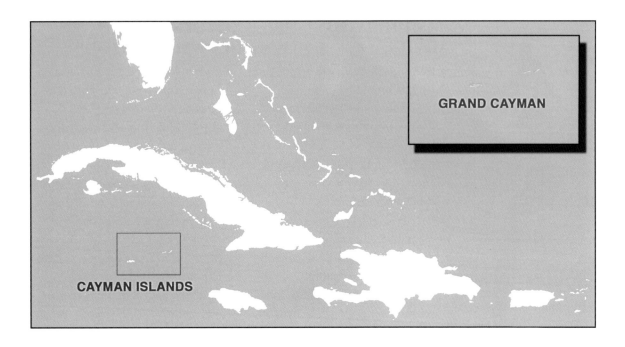

IMMUNISATION ADVICE

- Immunisations recommended in Britain should be up to date, especially those for children and tetanus boosters for adults.
- A course or booster of hepatitis A vaccine is usually advised.
- Vaccines sometimes recommended are: typhoid, tuberculosis, diphtheria, and hepatitis B.
- No certificate of vaccination for yellow fever is required.
- Malaria is not normally present.

OTHER HEALTH CONSIDERATIONS

- Water, food, and personal hygiene advice (including prevention of travellers' diarrhoea)
- Insect bite avoidance (to reduce risk of dengue)
- Avoidance of animal bites
- Sun and heat precautions
- Accident risks
- Risks associated with casual sex and prevention of blood-borne infections
- Full medical insurance

WEATHER – Grand Cayman

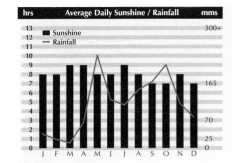

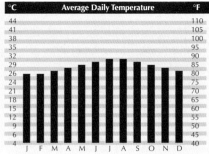

CENTRAL AFRICAN REPUBLIC

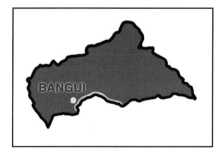

MALARIA ADVICE

- Malaria is a serious and sometimes fatal disease transmitted by mosquitoes. There is no vaccine available for malaria.

Malaria Precautions

- Malaria precautions are essential in all areas, all year round. Avoid mosquito bites by covering up with clothing (long sleeves and long trousers) especially after sunset, using insect repellents on exposed skin, and, when necessary, sleeping under an impregnated mosquito net.

- Check with your doctor or nurse about suitable antimalarial tablets.
- Prompt investigation of fever is essential. A person travelling to remote areas should carry, for emergency, standby treatment.

IMMUNISATION ADVICE

- Immunisations recommended in Britain should be up to date, especially those for children and poliomyelitis and tetanus boosters for adults.
- Courses or boosters of diphtheria, hepatitis A, typhoid and yellow fever vaccines are usually advised.
- Vaccines sometimes recommended are: hepatitis B, rabies, tuberculosis, and meningococcal A and C.

- A certificate of vaccination for yellow fever is mandatory as a condition of entry for anyone over 1 year of age.

OTHER HEALTH CONSIDERATIONS

- Water, food, and personal hygiene advice (including prevention of travellers' diarrhoea)
- Insect bite avoidance
- Avoidance of animal bites (to lessen the risk of rabies)
- Other hazards such as bilharzia
- Sun and heat precautions
- Accident risks (possibility of carrying a sterile medical pack)
- Risks associated with casual sex and prevention of blood-borne infections
- Full medical insurance

WEATHER – Bangui

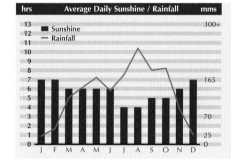

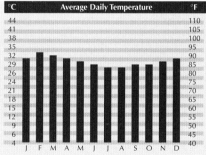

CHILE

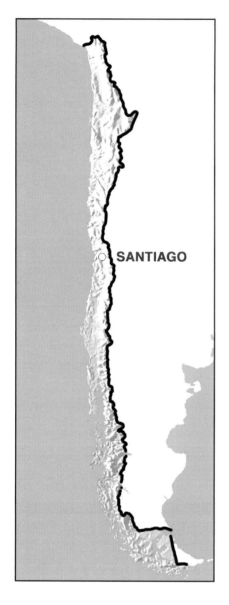

SANTIAGO

IMMUNISATION ADVICE

- Immunisations recommended in Britain should be up to date, especially those for children and tetanus boosters for adults.
- A course or booster of hepatitis A vaccine is usually advised.
- Vaccines sometimes recommended are: typhoid, rabies, hepatitis B, diphtheria, and tuberculosis.
- No certificate of vaccination for yellow fever is required.
- Malaria is not normally present.

OTHER HEALTH CONSIDERATIONS

- Water, food, and personal hygiene advice (including prevention of travellers' diarrhoea)
- Insect bite avoidance
- Avoidance of animal bites (to lessen the risk of rabies)
- Sun and heat precautions (in summer months)
- Accident risks (possibility of carrying a sterile medical pack)
- Risks associated with casual sex and prevention of blood-borne infections
- Full medical insurance

WEATHER – Santiago

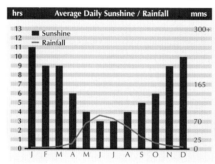

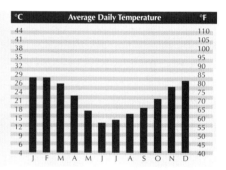

CHINA (INCLUDING TAIWAN)

MALARIA ADVICE

- Malaria is a serious and sometimes fatal disease transmitted by mosquitoes. There is no vaccine available for malaria.

Malaria Precautions

- Malaria precautions are essential in Hainan and Yunnan provinces, along the borders with Laos and Vietnam, Hainan Island. There is a very small risk in a few areas between the Yellow and Yangtze rivers. There is minimal risk in other areas including Taiwan. Avoid mosquito bites by covering up with clothing (long sleeves and long trousers) especially after sunset, using insect repellents on exposed skin, and, when necessary, sleeping under an impregnated mosquito net.

- Check with your doctor or nurse about suitable antimalarial tablets.
- Prompt investigation of fever is essential. A person travelling to remote areas should carry, for emergency, standby treatment.

IMMUNISATION ADVICE

- Immunisations recommended in Britain should be up to date, especially those for children and tetanus boosters for adults.

- Courses or boosters of diphtheria, hepatitis A and typhoid vaccines are usually advised.
- Vaccines sometimes recommended are: Japanese B encephalitis, rabies (China only), tuberculosis, hepatitis B, and poliomyelitis.
- A certificate of vaccination for yellow fever is required if entering from an infected area.

OTHER HEALTH CONSIDERATIONS

- Water, food, and personal hygiene advice (including prevention of travellers' diarrhoea)
- Insect bite avoidance (to reduce risk of dengue)
- Avoidance of animal bites (to lessen the risk of rabies)
- Other hazards such as bilharzia
- Sun and heat precautions
- Accident risks (possibility of carrying a sterile medical pack)
- Risks associated with casual sex and prevention of blood-borne infections
- Full medical insurance

WEATHER – Beijing

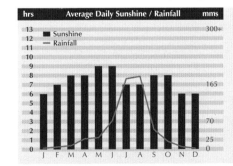

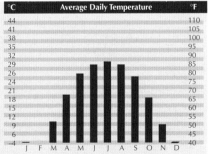

55

COLOMBIA

MALARIA ADVICE

- Malaria is a serious and sometimes fatal disease transmitted by mosquitoes. There is no vaccine available for malaria.

Malaria Precautions

- Malaria precautions are essential for all areas below 800 m, all year round. The risk is minimal in and around Bogota. Avoid mosquito bites by covering up with clothing (long sleeves and long trousers) especially after sunset, using insect repellents on exposed skin, and, when necessary, sleeping under an impregnated mosquito net.
- Check with your doctor or nurse about suitable antimalarial tablets.
- Prompt investigation of fever is essential. A person travelling to remote areas should carry, for emergency, standby treatment.

IMMUNISATION ADVICE

- Immunisations recommended in Britain should be up to date, especially those for children and tetanus boosters for adults.
- Courses or boosters of typhoid, yellow fever, and hepatitis A vaccines are usually advised.
- Vaccines sometimes recommended are: rabies, hepatitis B, tuberculosis, and diphtheria.
- No certificate of vaccination for yellow fever is required.

OTHER HEALTH CONSIDERATIONS

- Water, food, and personal hygiene advice (including prevention of travellers' diarrhoea)
- Insect bite avoidance (to reduce risk of dengue)
- Avoidance of animal bites (to lessen the risk of rabies)
- Sun and heat precautions
- Accident risks (possibility of carrying a sterile medical pack)
- Risks associated with casual sex and prevention of blood-borne infections
- Full medical insurance

WEATHER – Bogota

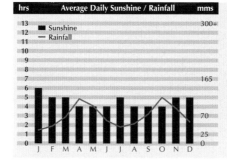

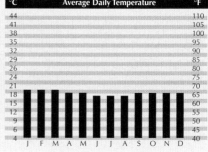

COSTA RICA

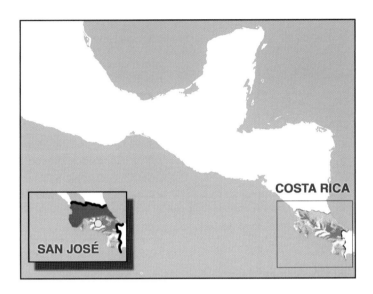

SAN JOSÉ

COSTA RICA

MALARIA ADVICE

- Malaria is a serious and some-times fatal disease transmitted by mosquitoes. There is no vaccine available for malaria.

Malaria Precautions

- Malaria precautions are essential in rural areas below 700 m in Alajuela, Guanacaste, Limón, and Heredia all year round. Avoid mosquito bites by covering up with clothing (long sleeves and long trousers) especially after sunset, using insect repellents on exposed skin, and, when necessary, sleeping under an impregnated mosquito net.
- Check with your doctor or nurse about suitable antimalarial tablets.
- Prompt investigation of fever is essential.

IMMUNISATION ADVICE

- Immunisations recommended in Britain should be up to date, especially those for children and tetanus boosters for adults.
- Courses or boosters of hepatitis A and typhoid vaccines are usually advised.

- Vaccines sometimes recom-mended are: tuberculosis, hepatitis B, rabies, and diphtheria.
- No certificate of vaccination for yellow fever is required.

OTHER HEALTH CONSIDERATIONS

- Water, food, and personal hygiene advice (including prevention of travellers' diarrhoea)
- Insect bite avoidance (to reduce risk of dengue)
- Avoidance of animal bites (to lessen the risk of rabies)
- Sun and heat precautions
- Accident risks (possibility of carrying a sterile medical pack)
- Risks associated with casual sex and prevention of blood-borne infections
- Full medical insurance

WEATHER – San José

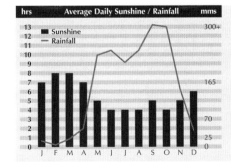

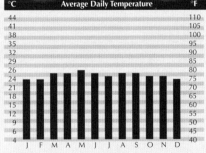

CROATIA

- No certificate of vaccination for yellow fever is required.
- Malaria is not normally present.

OTHER HEALTH CONSIDERATIONS

- Water, food, and personal hygiene advice (including prevention of travellers' diarrhoea)
- Insect bite avoidance
- Avoidance of animal bites (to lessen the risk of rabies)
- Sun and heat precautions (in summer months)
- Accident risks (possibility of carrying a sterile medical pack)
- Risks associated with casual sex and prevention of blood-borne infections
- Full medical insurance

IMMUNISATION ADVICE

- Immunisations recommended in Britain should be up to date, especially those for children and tetanus boosters for adults.
- Coursed or boosters of hepatitis A and diphtheria vaccines are usually advised.

- Vaccines sometimes recommended are: poliomyelitis, typhoid, hepatitis B, tuberculosis, tick-borne encephalitis, and rabies

WEATHER – Dubrovnik

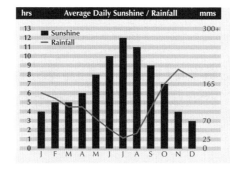

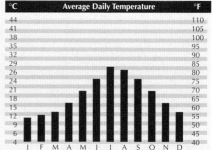

CUBA

HAVANA

OTHER HEALTH CONSIDERATIONS

- Water, food, and personal hygiene advice (including prevention of travellers' diarrhoea)
- Insect bite avoidance (to reduce risk of dengue)
- Avoidance of animal bites (to lessen the risk of rabies)
- Sun and heat precautions
- Accident risks (possibility of carrying a sterile medical pack)
- Risks associated with casual sex and prevention of blood-borne infections
- Full medical insurance

IMMUNISATION ADVICE

- Immunisations recommended in Britain should be up to date, especially those for children and tetanus boosters for adults.
- Courses or boosters of hepatitis A and typhoid vaccines are usually advised.
- Vaccines sometimes recommended are: tuberculosis, hepatitis B, rabies, and diphtheria.

- No certificate of vaccination for yellow fever is required.
- Malaria is not normally present.

WEATHER – Havana

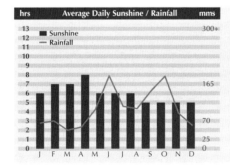

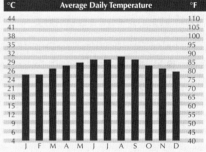

DEMOCRATIC REPUBLIC OF CONGO

MALARIA ADVICE

- Malaria is a serious and sometimes fatal disease transmitted by mosquitoes. There is no vaccine available for malaria.

Malaria Precautions

- Malaria precautions are essential in all areas, all year round. Avoid mosquito bites by covering up with clothing (long sleeves and long trousers) especially after sunset, using insect repellents on exposed skin, and, when necessary, sleeping under an impregnated mosquito net.
- Check with your doctor or nurse about suitable antimalarial tablets.

- Prompt investigation of fever is essential. A person travelling to remote areas should carry, for emergency, standby treatment.

IMMUNISATION ADVICE

- Immunisations recommended in Britain should be up to date, especially those for children and tetanus boosters for adults.
- Courses or boosters of diphtheria, hepatitis A, typhoid, and yellow fever vaccinations are usually advised.
- Vaccines sometimes recommended are: tuberculosis, hepatitis B, poliomyelitis, meningococcal A and C, and rabies.

- A certificate of vaccination for yellow fever is mandatory as a condition of entry for anyone over 1 year of age.

OTHER HEALTH CONSIDERATIONS

- Water, food, and personal hygiene advice (including prevention of travellers' diarrhoea)
- Insect bite avoidance
- Avoidance of animal bites (to lessen the risk of rabies)
- Other hazards such as bilharzia
- Sun and heat precautions
- Accident risks (possibility of carrying a sterile medical pack)
- Risks associated with casual sex and prevention of blood-borne infections
- Full medical insurance

WEATHER – Kinshasa

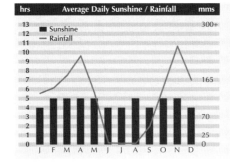

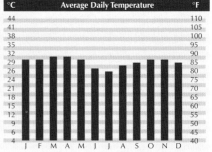

DOMINICA

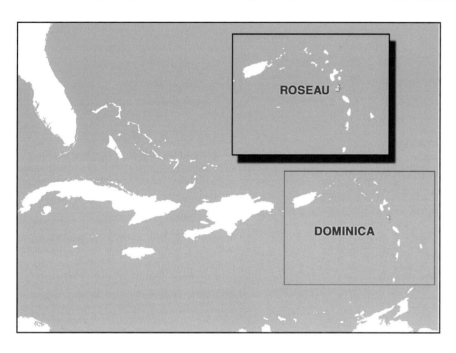

OTHER HEALTH CONSIDERATIONS

- Water, food, and personal hygiene advice (including prevention of travellers' diarrhoea)
- Insect bite avoidance (to reduce risk of dengue)
- Avoidance of animal bites
- Sun and heat precautions
- Accident risks (possibility of carrying a sterile medical pack)
- Risks associated with casual sex and prevention of blood-borne infections
- Full medical insurance

IMMUNISATION ADVICE

- Immunisations recommended in Britain should be up to date, especially those for children and tetanus boosters for adults.
- Courses or boosters of hepatitis A and typhoid vaccines are usually advised.
- Vaccines sometimes recommended are: diphtheria, hepatitis B, and tuberculosis.
- A certificate of vaccination for yellow fever is required for anyone over 1 year of age and entering from an infected area.
- Malaria is not normally present.

WEATHER – Roseau

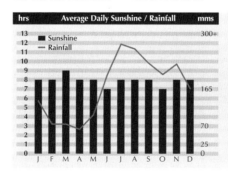

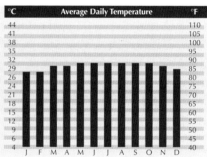

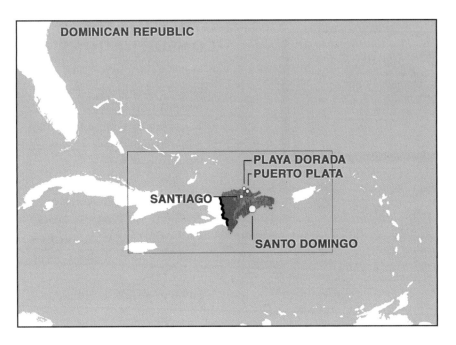

DOMINICAN REPUBLIC

PLAYA DORADA
PUERTO PLATA
SANTIAGO
SANTO DOMINGO

- Vaccines sometimes recommended are: tuberculosis, hepatitis B, and rabies.
- No certificate of vaccination for yellow fever is required.

OTHER HEALTH CONSIDERATIONS

- Water, food, and personal hygiene advice (including prevention of travellers' diarrhoea)
- Insect bite avoidance (to reduce risk of dengue)
- Avoidance of animal bites (to lessen the risk of rabies)
- Other hazards such as bilharzia
- Sun and heat precautions
- Accident risks (possibility of carrying a sterile medical pack)
- Risks associated with casual sex and prevention of blood-borne infections
- Full medical insurance

MALARIA ADVICE

- Malaria is a serious and sometimes fatal disease transmitted by mosquitoes. There is no vaccine available for malaria.

Malaria Precautions

- Malaria precautions are essential in all areas, all year round, although risk is less in tourist areas. Avoid mosquito bites by covering up with clothing (long sleeves and long trousers) especially after sunset, using insect repellents on exposed skin, and, when necessary, sleeping under an impregnated mosquito net.
- Check with your doctor or nurse about suitable antimalarial tablets.
- Prompt investigation of fever is essential. A person travelling to remote areas should carry, for emergency, standby treatment.

IMMUNISATION ADVICE

- Immunisations recommended in Britain should be up to date, especially those for children and tetanus boosters for adults.
- Courses or boosters of diphtheria, hepatitis A, and typhoid vaccines are usually advised.

WEATHER – Santo Domingo

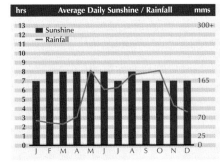

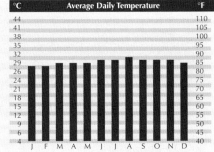

ECUADOR (INCLUDING THE GALAPAGOS ISLANDS)

MALARIA ADVICE

- Malaria is a serious and sometimes fatal disease transmitted by mosquitoes. There is no vaccine available for malaria.

Malaria Precautions

- Malaria precautions are essential in most areas below 1500 m, all year round. There is no risk in Guayaquil, Quito, or the Galapagos Islands. Avoid mosquito bites by covering up with clothing (long sleeves and long trousers) especially after sunset, using insect repellents on exposed skin, and, when necessary, sleeping under an impregnated mosquito net.
- Check with your doctor or nurse about suitable antimalarial tablets.

- Prompt investigation of fever is essential. A person travelling to remote areas should carry, for emergency, standby treatment.

IMMUNISATION ADVICE

- Immunisations recommended in Britain should be up to date, especially those for children and tetanus boosters for adults.
- Courses or boosters of diphtheria, hepatitis A, typhoid and yellow fever vaccines are usually advised.
- Vaccines sometimes recommended are: rabies, hepatitis B, and tuberculosis.
- A certificate of vaccination for yellow fever is required for anyone over 1 year of age and entering from an infected area.

OTHER HEALTH CONSIDERATIONS

- Water, food, and personal hygiene advice (including prevention of travellers' diarrhoea)
- Insect bite avoidance (to reduce risk of dengue)
- Avoidance of animal bites (to lessen the risk of rabies)
- Sun and heat precautions
- Accident risks (possibility of carrying a sterile medical pack)
- Risks associated with casual sex and prevention of blood-borne infections
- Full medical insurance

WEATHER – Quito

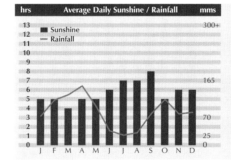

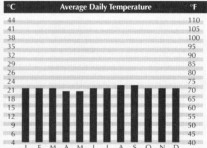

EGYPT

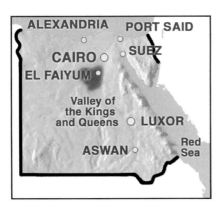

MALARIA ADVICE

- Malaria is a serious and sometimes fatal disease transmitted by mosquitoes. There is no vaccine available for malaria.

Malaria Precautions

- Malaria precautions are essential in the El Faiyûm area (50 miles south of Cairo on the west bank of the Nile) from June to October. Risk is minimal in other areas and tourist resorts. Avoid mosquito bites by covering up with clothing (long sleeves and long trousers) especially after sunset, using insect repellents on exposed skin, and, when necessary, sleeping under an impregnated mosquito net.
- Check with your doctor or nurse about suitable antimalarial tablets.
- Prompt investigation of fever is essential.

IMMUNISATION ADVICE

- Immunisations recommended in Britain should be up to date, especially those for children and poliomyelitis and tetanus boosters for adults.
- Courses or boosters of diphtheria, hepatitis A, typhoid vaccines are usually advised.
- Vaccines sometimes recommended are: tuberculosis, rabies, and hepatitis B.
- A certificate of vaccination for yellow fever is required for anyone over 1 year of age and entering from an infected area. Passengers from yellow fever–infected countries may be detained in the airport if they do not have a vaccination certificate.

OTHER HEALTH CONSIDERATIONS

- Water, food, and personal hygiene advice (including prevention of travellers' diarrhoea)
- Insect bite avoidance
- Avoidance of animal bites (to lessen the risk of rabies)
- Other hazards such as bilharzia
- Sun and heat precautions
- Accident risks (possibility of carrying a sterile medical pack)
- Risks associated with casual sex and prevention of blood-borne infections
- Full medical insurance

WEATHER – Luxor

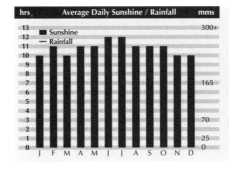

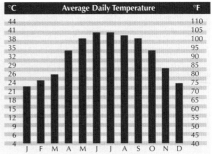

64

ETHIOPIA

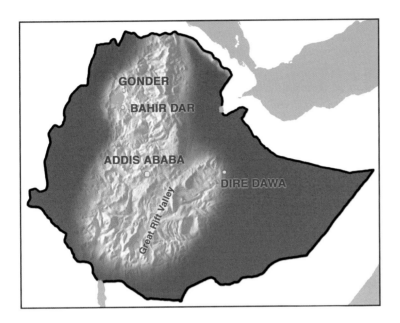

MALARIA ADVICE

- Malaria is a serious and sometimes fatal disease transmitted by mosquitoes. There is no vaccine available for malaria.

Malaria Precautions

- Malaria precautions are essential in all areas below 2,000 m, all year round. There is no risk in Addis Ababa. Avoid mosquito bites by covering up with clothing (long sleeves and long trousers) especially after sunset, using insect repellents on exposed skin, and, when necessary, sleeping under an impregnated mosquito net.
- Check with your doctor or nurse about suitable antimalarial tablets.

- Prompt investigation of fever is essential. A person travelling to remote areas should carry, for emergency, standby treatment.

IMMUNISATION ADVICE

- Immunisations recommended in Britain should be up to date, especially those for children and poliomyelitis and tetanus boosters for adults.

- Courses or boosters of diphtheria, hepatitis A, typhoid and yellow fever vaccines are usually advised.
- Vaccines sometimes recommended are: tuberculosis, meningococcal A and C, hepatitis B, and rabies.
- A certificate of vaccination for yellow fever is required for anyone over 1 year of age and entering from an infected area.

OTHER HEALTH CONSIDERATIONS

- Water, food, and personal hygiene advice (including prevention of travellers' diarrhoea)
- Insect bite avoidance
- Avoidance of animal bites (to lessen the risk of rabies)
- Other hazards such as bilharzia
- Sun and heat precautions
- Accident risks (possibility of carrying a sterile medical pack)
- Risks associated with casual sex and prevention of blood-borne infections
- Full medical insurance

WEATHER – Addis Ababa

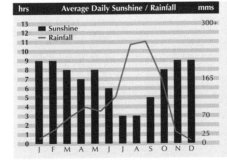

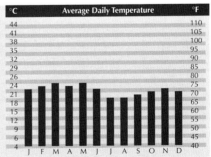

FIJI

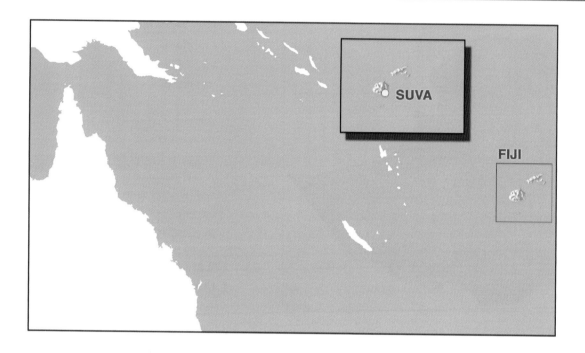

IMMUNISATION ADVICE

- Immunisations recommended in Britain should be up to date, especially those for children and tetanus boosters for adults.
- Courses or boosters of hepatitis A and typhoid vaccines are usually advised.
- Vaccines sometimes recommended are: diphtheria, and hepatitis B, tuberculosis, poliomyelitis.
- A certificate of vaccination for yellow fever is required for anyone over 1 year of age and entering Fiji within 10 days of have stayed overnight or longer in an infected area.
- Malaria is not normally present.

OTHER HEALTH CONSIDERATIONS

- Water, food, and personal hygiene advice (including prevention of travellers' diarrhoea)
- Insect bite avoidance (to reduce risk of dengue)
- Avoidance of animal bites
- Sun and heat precautions
- Accident risks (possibility of carrying a sterile medical pack)
- Risks associated with casual sex and prevention of blood-borne infections
- Full medical insurance

WEATHER – Suva

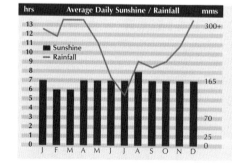

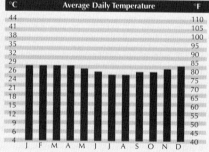

GAMBIA

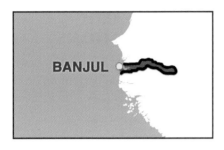

MALARIA ADVICE

- Malaria is a serous and some-times fatal disease transmitted by mosquitoes. There is no vaccine available for malaria.

Malaria Precautions

- Malaria precautions are essential in all areas, all year round. Avoid mosquito bites by covering up with clothing (long sleeves and long trousers) especially after sunset, using insect repellents on exposed skin, and, when necessary, sleeping under an impregnated mosquito net.
- Check with your doctor or nurse about suitable antimalarial tablets.
- Prompt investigation of fever is essential. A person travelling to remote areas should carry, for emergency, standby treatment.

IMMUNISATION ADVICE

- Immunisations recommended in Britain should be up to date, especially those for children and tetanus boosters for adults.
- Courses or boosters of diphtheria, hepatitis A, typhoid, and yellow fever vaccines are usually advised.
- Vaccines sometimes recommended are: hepatitis B, rabies, poliomyelitis, tuberculosis, and meningococcal A and C.
- A certificate of vaccination for yellow fever is required for anyone over 1 year of age and entering from an infected area.

OTHER HEALTH CONSIDERATIONS

- Water, food, and personal hygiene advice (including prevention of travellers' diarrhoea)
- Insect bite avoidance
- Avoidance of animal bites (to lessen the risk of rabies)
- Other hazards such as bilharzia
- Sun and heat precautions
- Accident risks (possibility of carrying a sterile medical pack)
- Risks associated with casual sex and prevention of blood-borne infections
- Full medical insurance

WEATHER – Banjul

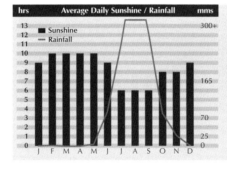

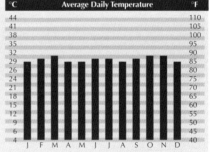

GHANA

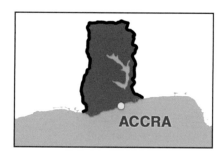

ACCRA

MALARIA ADVICE

- Malaria is a serious and some-times fatal disease transmitted by mosquitoes. There is no vaccine available for malaria.

Malaria Precautions

- Malaria precautions are essential in all areas, all year round. Avoid mosquito bites by covering up with clothing (long sleeves and long trousers) especially after sunset, using insect repellents on exposed skin, and, when necessary, sleeping under an impregnated mosquito net.
- Check with your doctor or nurse about suitable antimalarial tablets.
- Prompt investigation of fever is essential. A person travelling to remote areas should carry, for emergency, standby treatment.

IMMUNISATION ADVICE

- Immunisations recommended in Britain should be up to date, especially those for children and poliomyelitis and tetanus boosters for adults.
- Courses or boosters of diphtheria, hepatitis A, typhoid and yellow fever vaccines are usually advised.
- Vaccines sometimes recommended are: hepatitis B, rabies, tuberculosis, and meningococcal A and C (mainly in the North).
- A certificate of vaccination for yellow fever is mandatory as a condition of entry.

OTHER HEALTH CONSIDERATIONS

- Water, food, and personal hygiene advice (including prevention of travellers' diarrhoea)
- Insect bite avoidance
- Avoidance of animal bites (to lessen the risk of rabies)
- Other hazards such as bilharzia
- Sun and heat precautions
- Accident risks (possibility of carrying a sterile medical pack)
- Risks associated with casual sex and prevention of blood-borne infections
- Full medical insurance

WEATHER – Accra

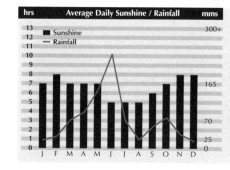

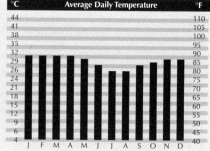

GRENADA

ST. GEORGE'S

GRENADA

OTHER HEALTH CONSIDERATIONS

- Water, food, and personal hygiene advice (including prevention of travellers' diarrhoea)
- Insect bite avoidance (to reduce risk of dengue)
- Avoidance of animal bites (to lessen the risk of rabies)
- Sun and heat precautions
- Accident risks (possibility of carrying a sterile medical pack)
- Risks associated with casual sex and prevention of blood-borne infections
- Full medical insurance

IMMUNISATION ADVICE

- Immunisations recommended in Britain should be up to date, especially those for children and tetanus boosters for adults.
- A course or booster of hepatitis A vaccine is usually advised.
- Vaccines sometimes recommended are: typhoid, diphtheria, hepatitis B, tuberculosis, and rabies.
- A certificate of vaccination for yellow fever is required for anyone over 1 year of age and entering from an infected area.
- Malaria is not normally present.

WEATHER – St. George's

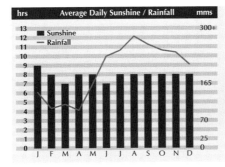

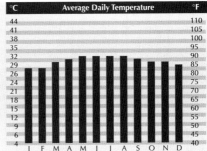

GUATEMALA

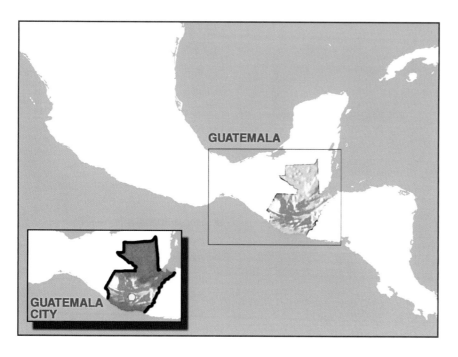

MALARIA ADVICE

- Malaria is a serious and sometimes fatal disease transmitted by mosquitoes. There is no vaccine available for malaria.

Malaria Precautions

- Malaria precautions are essential in all areas below 1,500 m, all year round. Avoid mosquito bites by covering up with clothing (long sleeves and long trousers) especially after sunset, using insect repellents on exposed skin, and, when necessary, sleeping under an impregnated mosquito net.
- Check with your doctor or nurse about suitable antimalarial tablets.
- Prompt investigation of fever is essential.

IMMUNISATION ADVICE

- Immunisations recommended in Britain should be up to date, especially those for children and tetanus boosters for adults.
- Courses or boosters of hepatitis A and typhoid vaccines are usually advised.

- Vaccines sometimes recommended are: rabies, hepatitis B, tuberculosis, and diphtheria.
- A certificate of vaccination for yellow fever is required for anyone over 1 year of age and entering from countries with an infected area.

OTHER HEALTH CONSIDERATIONS

- Water, food, and personal hygiene advice (including prevention of travellers' diarrhoea)
- Insect bite avoidance (to reduce risk of dengue)
- Avoidance of animal bites (to lessen the risk of rabies)
- Sun and heat precautions
- Accident risks (possibility of carrying a sterile medical pack)
- Risks associated with casual sex and prevention of blood-borne infections
- Full medical insurance

WEATHER – Guatemala City

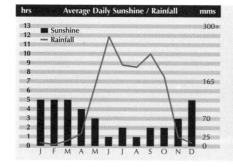

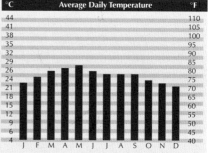

70

GUYANA

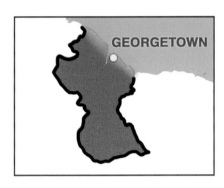

GEORGETOWN

MALARIA ADVICE

- Malaria is a serious and some-times fatal disease transmitted by mosquitoes. There is no vaccine available for malaria.

Malaria Precautions

- Malaria precautions are essential in all parts of the interior of the country, all year round. Sporadic cases are reported from the coastal belt. Avoid mosquito bites by covering up with clothing (long sleeves and long trousers) especially after sunset, using insect repellents on exposed skin, and, when necessary, sleeping under an impregnated mosquito net.
- Check with your doctor or nurse about suitable antimalarial tablets.

- Prompt investigation of fever is essential. A person travelling to remote areas should carry, for emergency, standby treatment.

IMMUNISATION ADVICE

- Immunisations recommended in Britain should be up to date, especially those for children and tetanus boosters for adults.
- Courses or boosters of hepatitis A, typhoid and yellow fever vaccines are usually advised.
- Vaccines sometimes recom-mended are: tuberculosis, hepatitis B, rabies, and diphtheria.
- A certificate of vaccination for yellow fever is required if entering from an infected area.

OTHER HEALTH CONSIDERATIONS

- Water, food, and personal hygiene advice (including prevention of travellers' diarrhoea)
- Insect bite avoidance (to reduce risk of dengue)
- Avoidance of animal bites (to lessen the risk of rabies)
- Other hazards such as bilharzia
- Sun and heat precautions
- Accident risks (possibility of carrying a sterile medical pack)
- Risks associated with casual sex and prevention of blood-borne infections
- Full medical insurance

WEATHER – Georgetown

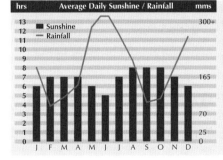

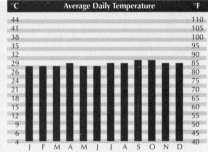

HAITI

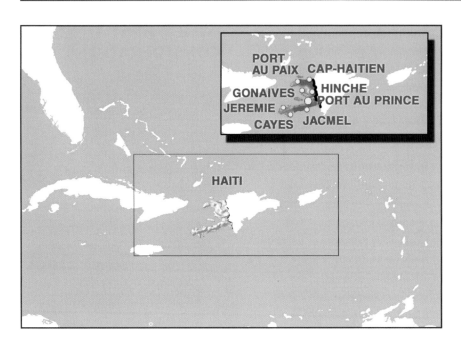

MALARIA ADVICE

- Malaria is a serous and sometimes fatal disease transmitted by mosquitoes. There is no vaccine available for malaria.

Malaria Precautions

- Malaria precautions are essential in the forest areas of Chantal, Gros Morne, Hinche, and Jacmel Maissade, all year round. The risk in other areas is low. Avoid mosquito bites by covering up with clothing (long sleeves and long trousers) especially after sunset, using insect repellents on exposed skin, and, when necessary, sleeping under an impregnated mosquito net.
- Check with your doctor or nurse about suitable antimalarial tablets.

- Prompt investigation of fever is essential. A person travelling to remote areas should carry, for emergency, standby treatment.

IMMUNISATION ADVICE

- Immunisations recommended in Britain should be up to date, especially those for children and tetanus boosters for adults.
- Courses or boosters of diphtheria, hepatitis A and typhoid vaccines are usually advised.
- Vaccines sometimes recommended are: tuberculosis, hepatitis B, and rabies.
- A certificate of vaccination for yellow fever is required if entering from an infected area.

OTHER HEALTH CONSIDERATIONS

- Water, food, and personal hygiene advice (including prevention of travellers' diarrhoea)
- Insect bite avoidance (to reduce risk of dengue)
- Avoidance of animal bites (to lessen the risk of rabies)
- Sun and heat precautions
- Accident risks (possibility of carrying a sterile medical pack)
- Risks associated with casual sex and prevention of blood-borne infections
- Full medical insurance

WEATHER – Port-au-Prince

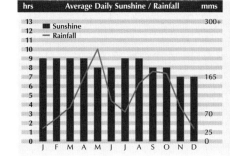

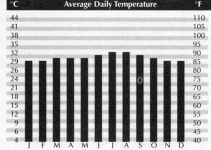

HONG KONG

MALARIA ADVICE

- Malaria is a serious and some-times fatal disease transmitted by mosquitoes. There is no vaccine available for malaria.

Malaria Precautions

- Malaria precautions are essential only in northern rural areas near China, all year round. Avoid mosquito bites when possible by covering up with clothing (long sleeves and long trousers) especially after sunset, using insect repellents on exposed skin, and, when necessary, sleeping under an impregnated mosquito net.

- Antimalarial tablets are not normally recommended.
- Prompt investigation of fever is essential.

IMMUNISATION ADVICE

- Immunisations recommended in Britain should be up to date, especially those for children and tetanus boosters for adults.
- Vaccines sometimes recom-mended are: hepatitis A, typhoid, hepatitis B, tuberculosis, diphtheria, and poliomyelitis.
- No certificate of vaccination for yellow fever is required.

OTHER HEALTH CONSIDERATIONS

- Water, food, and personal hygiene advice (including prevention of travellers' diarrhoea)
- Insect bite avoidance (to reduce risk of dengue)
- Avoidance of animal bites (to lessen the risk of rabies)
- Sun and heat precautions
- Accident risks
- Risks associated with casual sex and prevention of blood-borne infections
- Full medical insurance

WEATHER – Hong Kong

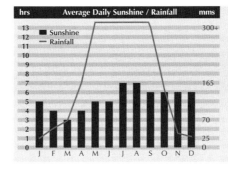

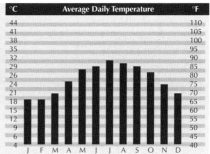

INDIA

MALARIA ADVICE

• Malaria is a serious and sometimes fatal disease transmitted by mosquitoes. There is no vaccine available for malaria.

Malaria Precautions

• Malaria precautions are essential in all areas below 2,000 m, all year round. There is no risk in Himachal Pradesh, Jammu, Kashmir, and Sikkim, which are at high altitude. Avoid mosquito bites by covering up with clothing (long sleeves and long trousers) especially after sunset, using insect repellents on exposed skin, and, when necessary, sleeping under an impregnated mosquito net.

• Check with your doctor or nurse about suitable antimalarial tablets.

• Prompt investigation of fever is essential. A person travelling to remote areas should carry, for emergency, standby treatment.

IMMUNISATION ADVICE

• Immunisations recommended in Britain should be up to date, especially those for children and poliomyelitis and tetanus boosters for adults.

• Courses or boosters of diphtheria, hepatitis A and typhoid vaccines are usually advised.

• Vaccines sometimes recommended are: hepatitis B, rabies, tuberculosis, and Japanese B encephalitis.

• A certificate of vaccination for yellow fever is required for anyone over 6 months of age and entering from or being in transit through an infected area within the previous 6 days.

OTHER HEALTH CONSIDERATIONS

• Water, food, and personal hygiene advice (including prevention of travellers' diarrhoea)

• Insect bite avoidance (to reduce risk of dengue)

• Avoidance of animal bites (to lessen the risk of rabies)

• Sun and heat precautions

• Accident risks (possibility of carrying a sterile medical pack)

• Risks associated with casual sex and prevention of blood-borne infections

• Full medical insurance

WEATHER – Delhi and Chennai

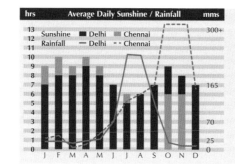

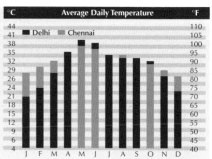

INDONESIA (INCLUDING BALI)

MALARIA ADVICE

- Malaria is a serious and sometimes fatal disease transmitted by mosquitoes. There is no vaccine available for malaria.

Malaria Precautions

- Malaria precautions are essential in all areas except the municipality of Jakarta, large cities, and the tourist resorts of Bali and Java, all year round. Avoid mosquito bites by covering up with clothing (long sleeves and long trousers) especially after sunset, using insect repellents on exposed skin, and, when necessary, sleeping under an impregnated mosquito net.
- Check with your doctor or nurse about suitable antimalarial tablets.
- Prompt investigation of fever is essential. A person travelling to remote areas should carry, for emergency, standby treatment.

IMMUNISATION ADVICE

- Immunisations recommended in Britain should be up to date, especially those for children and tetanus boosters for adults.
- Courses or boosters of diphtheria, hepatitis A and typhoid vaccines are usually advised.
- Vaccines sometimes recommended are: poliomyelitis, tuberculosis, hepatitis B, rabies, and Japanese B encephalitis.
- A certificate of vaccination for yellow fever is required if entering from an infected area.

OTHER HEALTH CONSIDERATIONS

- Water, food, and personal hygiene advice (including prevention of travellers' diarrhoea)
- Insect bite avoidance (to reduce risk of dengue)
- Avoidance of animal bites (to lessen the risk of rabies)
- Other hazards such as bilharzia
- Sun and heat precautions
- Accident risks (possibility of carrying a sterile medical pack)
- Risks associated with casual sex and prevention of blood-borne infections
- Full medical insurance

WEATHER – Jakarta

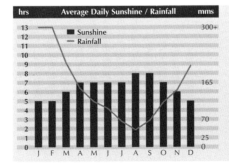

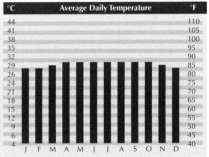

IRAN

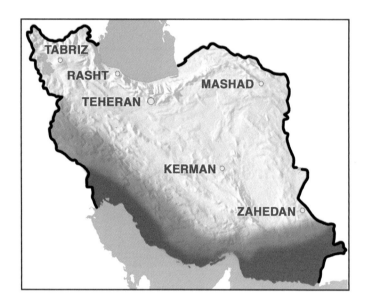

MALARIA ADVICE

- Malaria is a serious and sometimes fatal disease transmitted by mosquitoes. There is no vaccine available for malaria.

Malaria Precautions

- Malaria precautions are essential in areas north of the Zagros mountains and in western and southwestern regions, in the summer months and in the provinces of Sistan-Baluchestan, Hormozgan, and Kerman from March to November. Avoid mosquito bites by covering up with clothing (long sleeves and long trousers) especially after sunset, using insect repellents on exposed skin, and, when necessary, sleeping under an impregnated mosquito net.
- Check with your doctor or nurse about suitable antimalarial tablets.

- Prompt investigation of fever is essential. A person travelling to remote areas should carry, for emergency, standby treatment.

IMMUNISATION ADVICE

- Immunisations recommended in Britain should be up to date, especially those for children and poliomyelitis and tetanus boosters for adults.

- Courses or boosters of diphtheria, hepatitis A and typhoid vaccines are usually advised.
- Vaccines sometimes recommended are: rabies, hepatitis B, and tuberculosis.
- No certificate of vaccination for yellow fever is required.

OTHER HEALTH CONSIDERATIONS

- Water, food, and personal hygiene advice (including prevention of travellers' diarrhoea)
- Insect bite avoidance
- Avoidance of animal bites (to lessen the risk of rabies)
- Sun and heat precautions
- Accident risks (possibility of carrying a sterile medical pack)
- Risks associated with casual sex and prevention of blood-borne infections
- Full medical insurance

WEATHER – Tehran

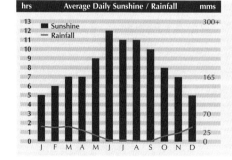

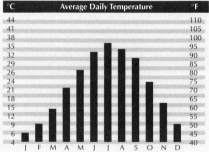

IRAQ

MALARIA ADVICE

- Malaria is a serious and sometimes fatal disease transmitted by mosquitoes. There is no vaccine available for malaria.

Malaria Precautions

- Malaria precautions are essential in northern rural areas below 1,500 m but also in Basrah province, from May to November. Avoid mosquito bites by covering up with clothing (long sleeves and long trousers) especially after sunset, using insect repellents on exposed skin, and, when necessary, sleeping under an impregnated mosquito net.
- Check with your doctor or nurse about suitable antimalarial tablets.
- Prompt investigation of fever is essential.

IMMUNISATION ADVICE

- Immunisations recommended in Britain should be up to date, especially those for children and poliomyelitis and tetanus boosters for adults.
- Courses or boosters of diphtheria, hepatitis A and typhoid vaccines are usually advised.
- Vaccines sometimes recommended are: rabies, hepatitis B, and tuberculosis.
- A certificate of vaccination for yellow fever is required for anyone entering from an infected area.

OTHER HEALTH CONSIDERATIONS

- Water, food, and personal hygiene advice (including prevention of travellers' diarrhoea)
- Insect bite avoidance
- Avoidance of animal bites (to lessen the risk of rabies)
- Other hazards such as bilharzia
- Sun and heat precautions
- Accident risks (possibility of carrying a sterile medical pack)
- Risks associated with casual sex and prevention of blood-borne infections
- Full medical insurance

WEATHER – Baghdad

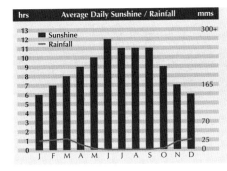

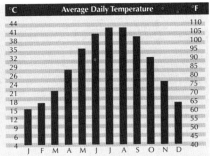

ISRAEL

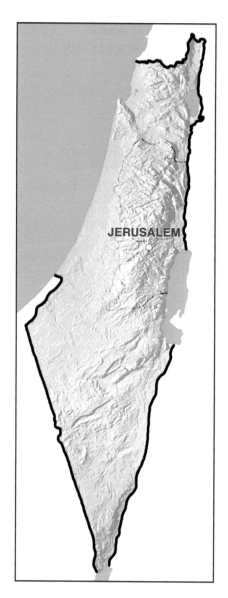

IMMUNISATION ADVICE

- Immunisations recommended in Britain should be up to date, especially those for children and tetanus boosters for adults.
- A course or booster of hepatitis A vaccine is usually advised.
- Vaccines sometimes recommended are: tuberculosis, hepatitis B, diphtheria, typhoid, rabies, and poliomyelitis.
- No certificate of vaccination for yellow fever is required.
- Malaria is not normally present.

OTHER HEALTH CONSIDERATIONS

- Water, food, and personal hygiene advice (including prevention of travellers' diarrhoea)
- Insect bite avoidance
- Avoidance of animal bites (to lessen the risk of rabies)
- Sun and heat precautions
- Accident risks (possibility of carrying a sterile medical pack)
- Risks associated with casual sex and prevention of blood-borne infections
- Full medical insurance

WEATHER – Jerusalem

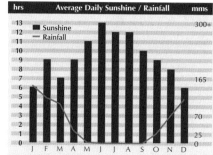

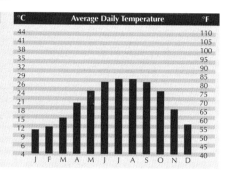

JAMAICA

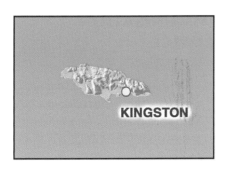

KINGSTON

OTHER HEALTH CONSIDERATIONS

- Water, food, and personal hygiene advice (including prevention of travellers' diarrhoea)
- Insect bite avoidance (to reduce risk of dengue)
- Avoidance of animal bites
- Sun and heat precautions
- Accident risks
- Risks associated with casual sex and prevention of blood-borne infections
- Full medical insurance

IMMUNISATION ADVICE

- Immunisations recommended in Britain should be up to date, especially those for children and tetanus boosters for adults.
- A course or booster of hepatitis A vaccine is usually advised.
- Vaccines sometimes recommended are: typhoid, tuberculosis, diphtheria, and hepatitis B.
- A certificate of vaccination for yellow fever is required for anyone over 1 year of age and entering from an infected area.
- Malaria is not normally present.

WEATHER – Kingston

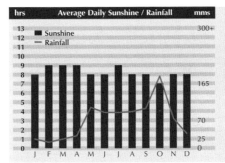

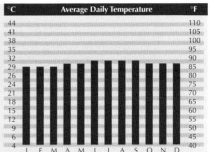

JAPAN

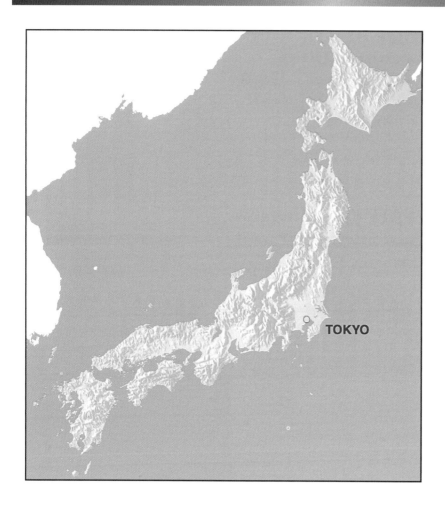

TOKYO

IMMUNISATION ADVICE

- Immunisations recommended in Britain should be up to date, especially those for children.
- Vaccine sometimes recommended is: Japanese B encephalitis.
- No certificate of vaccination for yellow fever is required.
- Malaria is not normally present.

OTHER HEALTH CONSIDERATIONS

- Insect bite avoidance
- Avoidance of animal bites
- Other hazards such as bilharzia
- Sun and heat precautions (in summer months)
- Accident risks
- Risks associated with casual sex and prevention of blood-borne infections
- Full medical insurance

WEATHER – Tokyo

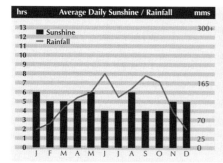

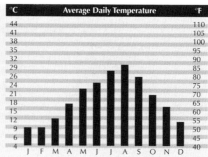

KENYA

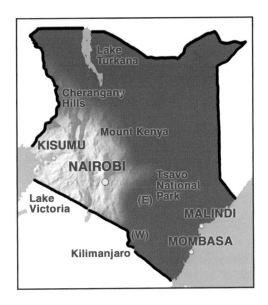

MALARIA ADVICE

- Malaria is a serious and some-times fatal disease transmitted by mosquitoes. There is no vaccine available for malaria.

Malaria Precautions

- Malaria precautions are essential in all areas all year round, although the risk is small in Nairobi and the highlands (above 2,500 m). Avoid mosquito bites by covering up with clothing (long sleeves and long trousers) especially after sunset, using insect repellents on exposed skin, and, when necessary, sleeping under an impregnated mosquito net.
- Check with your doctor or nurse about suitable antimalarial tablets.
- Prompt investigation of fever is essential. A person travelling to remote areas should carry, for emergency, standby treatment.

IMMUNISATION ADVICE

- Immunisations recommended in Britain should be up to date, especially those for children and tetanus boosters for adults.
- Courses or boosters of diphtheria, hepatitis A, typhoid and yellow fever vaccines are usually advised.

- Vaccines sometimes recom-mended are: meningococcal A and C, poliomyelitis, hepatitis B, rabies, and tuberculosis.
- A certificate of vaccination for yellow fever is required for anyone over 1 year of age and entering from an infected area.

OTHER HEALTH CONSIDERATIONS

- Water, food, and personal hygiene advice (including prevention of travellers' diarrhoea)
- Insect bite avoidance (to reduce risk of dengue)
- Avoidance of animal bites (to lessen the risk of rabies)
- Other hazards such as bilharzia
- Sun and heat precautions
- Accident risks (possibility of carrying a sterile medical pack)
- Risks associated with casual sex and prevention of blood-borne infections
- Full medical insurance

WEATHER – Mombasa

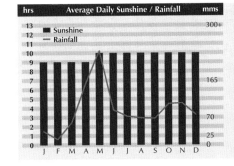

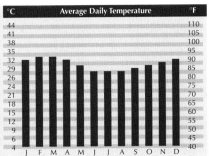

KOREA, DEMOCRATIC PEOPLES REPUBLIC OF (NORTH KOREA)

MALARIA ADVICE

- Malaria is a serious and sometimes fatal disease transmitted by mosquitoes. There is no vaccine available for malaria.

Malaria Precautions

- Malaria precautions are essential in some southern areas all year round. Avoid mosquito bites by covering up with clothing (long sleeves and long trousers) especially after sunset, using insect repellents on exposed skin, and, when necessary, sleeping under an impregnated mosquito net.
- Check with your doctor or nurse about suitable antimalarial tablets.
- Prompt investigation of fever is essential.

IMMUNISATION ADVICE

- Immunisations recommended in Britain should be up to date, especially those for children and tetanus boosters for adults.
- A course or booster of hepatitis A vaccine is usually advised.
- Vaccines sometimes recommended are: diphtheria, tuberculosis, poliomyelitis, hepatitis B, Japanese B encephalitis, and rabies.
- No certificate of vaccination for yellow fever is required.

OTHER HEALTH CONSIDERATIONS

- Water, food, and personal hygiene advice (including prevention of travellers' diarrhoea)
- Insect bite avoidance (to reduce risk of dengue)
- Avoidance of animal bites (to lessen the risk of rabies)
- Sun and heat precautions
- Accident risks (possibility of carrying a sterile medical pack)
- Risks associated with casual sex and prevention of blood-borne infections
- Full medical insurance

WEATHER – Pyongyang

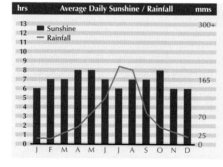

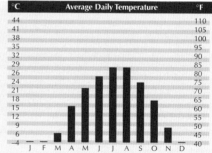

KOREA, REPUBLIC OF (SOUTH KOREA)

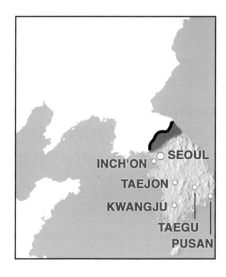

MALARIA ADVICE

- Malaria is a serious and sometimes fatal disease transmitted by mosquitoes. There is no vaccine available for malaria.

Malaria Precautions

- Malaria precautions are essential in rural areas in the far north of the country, all year round. Avoid mosquito bites by covering up with clothing (long sleeves and long trousers) especially after sunset, using insect repellents on exposed skin, and, when necessary, sleeping under an impregnated mosquito net.
- Check with your doctor or nurse about suitable antimalarial tablets.
- Prompt investigation of fever is essential.

IMMUNISATION ADVICE

- Immunisations recommended in Britain should be up to date, especially those for children and tetanus boosters for adults.
- A course or booster of hepatitis A vaccine is usually advised.
- Vaccines sometimes recommended are: diphtheria, tuberculosis, hepatitis B, Japanese B encephalitis, typhoid, rabies, and poliomyelitis.
- No certificate of vaccination for yellow fever is required.

OTHER HEALTH CONSIDERATIONS

- Water, food, and personal hygiene advice (including prevention of travellers' diarrhoea)
- Insect bite avoidance (to reduce risk of dengue)
- Avoidance of animal bites (to lessen the risk of rabies)
- Sun and heat precautions
- Accident risks (possibility of carrying a sterile medical pack)
- Risks associated with casual sex and prevention of blood-borne infections
- Full medical insurance

WEATHER – Seoul

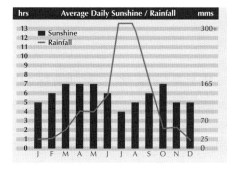

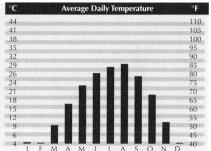

LAO PEOPLE'S DEMOCRATIC REPUBLIC

VIENTIANE

MALARIA ADVICE

• Malaria is a serious and some-times fatal disease transmitted by mosquitoes. There is no vaccine available for malaria.

Malaria Precautions

• Malaria precautions are essential in all areas (except Vientiane and at high altitude where the risk is minimal) all year round. Avoid mosquito bites by covering up with clothing (long sleeves and long trousers) especially after sunset, using insect repellents on exposed skin, and, when necessary, sleeping under an impregnated mosquito net.

• Check with your doctor or nurse about suitable antimalarial tablets.
• Prompt investigation of fever is essential. A person travelling to remote areas should carry, for emergency, standby treatment.

IMMUNISATION ADVICE

• Immunisations recommended in Britain should be up to date, especially those for children and tetanus boosters for adults.
• Courses or boosters of hepatitis A diptheria, and typhoid vaccines are usually advised.
• Vaccines sometimes recommended are: tuberculosis, rabies, hepatitis B, Japanese B encephalitis, and poliomyelitis.

• A certificate of vaccination for yellow fever is required for anyone entering from an infected area.

OTHER HEALTH CONSIDERATIONS

• Water, food, and personal hygiene advice (including prevention of travellers' diarrhoea)
• Insect bite avoidance (to reduce risk of dengue)
• Avoidance of animal bites (to lessen the risk of rabies)
• Sun and heat precautions
• Accident risks (possibility of carrying a sterile medical pack)
• Risks associated with casual sex and prevention of blood-borne infections
• Full medical insurance

WEATHER – Vientiane

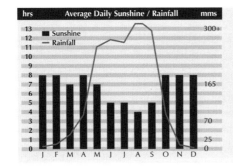

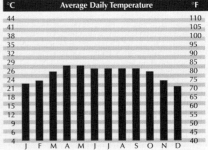

LATVIA

IMMUNISATION ADVICE

- Immunisations recommended in Britain should be up to date, especially those for children and tetanus boosters for adults.
- Coursed or boosters of hepatitis A and diphtheria vaccines are usually advised.
- Vaccines sometimes recommended are: poliomyelitis, tuberculosis, tick-borne encephalitis, hepatitis B, rabies, and typhoid.
- No certificate of vaccination for yellow fever is required.
- Malaria is not normally present.

OTHER HEALTH CONSIDERATIONS

- Water, food, and personal hygiene advice (including prevention of travellers' diarrhoea)
- Insect bite avoidance
- Avoidance of animal bites (to lessen the risk of rabies)
- Sun and heat precautions (in summer months)
- Accident risks (possibility of carrying a sterile medical pack)
- Risks associated with casual sex and prevention of blood-borne infections
- Full medical insurance

WEATHER – Riga

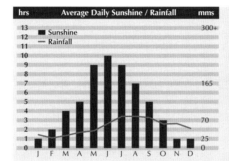

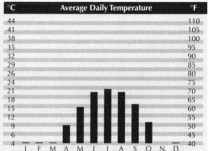

LITHUANIA

IMMUNISATION ADVICE

- Immunisations recommended in Britain should be up to date, especially those for children and tetanus boosters for adults.
- Coursed or boosters of hepatitis A and diphtheria vaccines are usually advised.
- Vaccines sometimes recommended are: poliomyelitis, typhoid, tuberculosis, rabies, tick-borne encephalitis, and hepatitis B.
- No certificate of vaccination for yellow fever is required.
- Malaria is not normally present.

OTHER HEALTH CONSIDERATIONS

- Water, food, and personal hygiene advice (including prevention of travellers' diarrhoea)
- Insect bite avoidance
- Avoidance of animal bites (to lessen the risk of rabies)
- Sun and heat precautions (in summer months)
- Accident risks (possibility of carrying a sterile medical pack)
- Risks associated with casual sex and prevention of blood-borne infections
- Full medical insurance

WEATHER – Vilnius

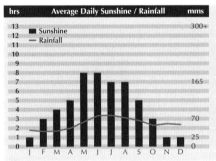

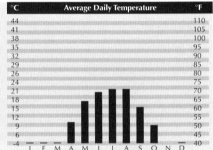

MALAWI

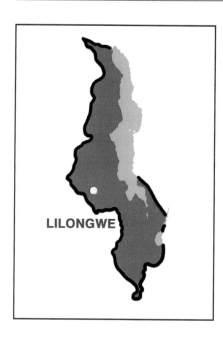

LILONGWE

MALARIA ADVICE

- Malaria is a serious and sometimes fatal disease transmitted by mosquitoes. There is no vaccine available for malaria.

Malaria Precautions

- Malaria precautions are essential in all areas, all year round. Avoid mosquito bites by covering up with clothing (long sleeves and long trousers) especially after sunset, using insect repellents on exposed skin, and, when necessary, sleeping under an impregnated mosquito net.

- Check with your doctor or nurse about suitable antimalarial tablets.
- Prompt investigation of fever is essential. A person travelling to remote areas should carry, for emergency, standby treatment.

IMMUNISATION ADVICE

- Immunisations recommended in Britain should be up to date, especially those for children and tetanus boosters for adults.
- Courses or boosters of diphtheria, hepatitis A and typhoid vaccines are usually advised.
- Vaccines sometimes recommended are: tuberculosis, hepatitis B, rabies, poliomyelitis, and meningococcal A and C.

- A certificate of vaccination for yellow fever is required for anyone entering from an infected area.

OTHER HEALTH CONSIDERATIONS

- Water, food, and personal hygiene advice (including prevention of travellers' diarrhoea)
- Insect bite avoidance
- Avoidance of animal bites (to lessen the risk of rabies)
- Other hazards such as bilharzia
- Sun and heat precautions
- Accident risks (possibility of carrying a sterile medical pack)
- Risks associated with casual sex and prevention of blood-borne infections
- Full medical insurance

WEATHER – Lilongwe

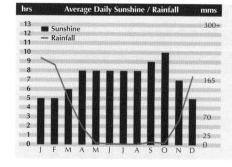

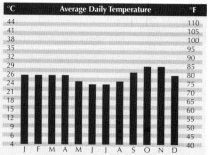

MALAYSIA

MALARIA ADVICE

- Malaria is a serious and some-times fatal disease transmitted by mosquitoes. There is no vaccine available for malaria.

Malaria Precautions

- Malaria precautions are essential for all of Sabah, all year round. In Sarawak and peninsular Malaysia, the risk is confined to inland forested regions, all year round. There is minimal risk in other areas. Avoid mosquito bites by covering up with clothing (long sleeves and long trousers) especially after sunset, using insect repellents on exposed skin, and, when necessary, sleeping under an impregnated mosquito net.
- Check with your doctor or nurse about suitable antimalarial tablets.
- Prompt investigation of fever is essential. A person travelling to remote areas should carry, for emergency, standby treatment.

IMMUNISATION ADVICE

- Immunisations recommended in Britain should be up to date, especially those for children and tetanus boosters for adults.
- Courses or boosters of hepatitis A and typhoid vaccines are usually advised.
- Vaccines sometimes recommended are: poliomyelitis, diphtheria, tuberculosis, rabies, hepatitis B, and Japanese B encephalitis (risk is minimal in western peninsular Malaysia).

- A certificate of vaccination for yellow fever is required for anyone over 1 year of age and entering from an infected area.

OTHER HEALTH CONSIDERATIONS

- Water, food, and personal hygiene advice (including prevention of travellers' diarrhoea)
- Insect bite avoidance (to reduce risk of dengue)
- Avoidance of animal bites (to lessen the risk of rabies)
- Sun and heat precautions
- Accident risks (possibility of carrying a sterile medical pack)
- Risks associated with casual sex and prevention of blood-borne infections
- Full medical insurance

WEATHER – Kuala Lumpur

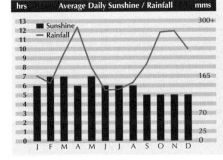

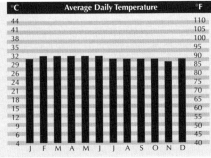

MALDIVES

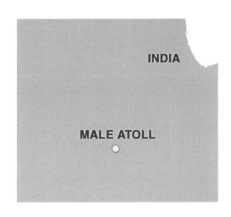

INDIA

MALE ATOLL

IMMUNISATION ADVICE

- Immunisations recommended in Britain should be up to date, especially those for children and tetanus boosters for adults.
- Courses or boosters of hepatitis A and typhoid vaccines are usually advised.

- Vaccines sometimes recommended are: diphtheria, tuberculosis, poliomyelitis, hepatitis B, and rabies.
- A certificate of vaccination for yellow fever is required for anyone entering from an infected area.
- Malaria is not normally present.

OTHER HEALTH CONSIDERATIONS

- Water, food, and personal hygiene advice (including prevention of travellers' diarrhoea)

- Insect bite avoidance (to reduce risk of dengue)
- Avoidance of animal bites (to lessen the risk of rabies)
- Sun and heat precautions
- Accident risks (possibility of carrying a sterile medical pack)
- Risks associated with casual sex and prevention of blood-borne infections
- Full medical insurance

WEATHER – Male Atoll

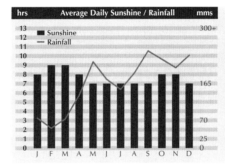

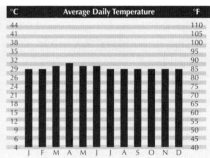

MAURITIUS

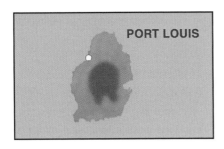

PORT LOUIS

MALARIA ADVICE

- Malaria is a serious and some-times fatal disease transmitted by mosquitoes. There is no vaccine available for malaria.

Malaria Precautions

- Malaria precautions are essential only in rural areas, all year round. There is no significant risk in other areas or on Rodriguez Island. Avoid mosquito bites by covering up with clothing (long sleeves and long trousers) especially after sunset, using insect repellents on exposed skin, and, when necessary, sleeping under an impregnated mosquito net.
- Check with your doctor or nurse about suitable antimalarial tablets.
- Prompt investigation of fever is essential.

IMMUNISATION ADVICE

- Immunisations recommended in Britain should be up to date, especially those for children and tetanus boosters for adults.
- Courses or boosters of diphtheria, hepatitis A and typhoid vaccines are usually advised.
- Vaccines sometimes recom-mended are: tuberculosis, rabies, poliomyelitis, and hepatitis B.
- A certificate of vaccination for yellow fever is required for anyone over 1 year of age and entering from an infected area.

OTHER HEALTH CONSIDERATIONS

- Water, food, and personal hygiene advice (including prevention of travellers' diarrhoea)
- Insect bite avoidance
- Avoidance of animal bites (to lessen the risk of rabies)
- Sun and heat precautions
- Accident risks (possibility of carrying a sterile medical pack)
- Risks associated with casual sex and prevention of blood-borne infections
- Full medical insurance

WEATHER – Port Louis

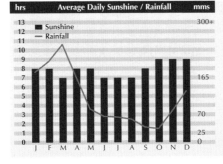

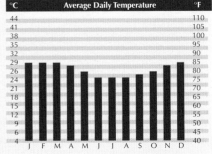

MEXICO

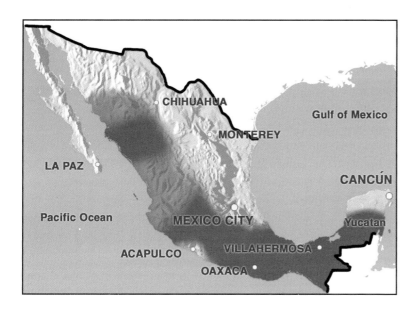

MALARIA ADVICE

- Malaria is a serious and sometimes fatal disease transmitted by mosquitoes. There is no vaccine available for malaria.

Malaria Precautions

- Malaria precautions are essential in some rural areas along the west coast and in the south of the country, all year round. Malaria is unusual in developed tourist resorts and the risk in Cancun is very small although the infection is present in nearby rural areas. Avoid mosquito bites by covering up with clothing (long sleeves and long trousers) especially after sunset, using insect repellents on exposed skin, and, when necessary, sleeping under an impregnated mosquito net.

- Check with your doctor or nurse about suitable antimalarial tablets.
- Prompt investigation of fever is essential.

IMMUNISATION ADVICE

- Immunisations recommended in Britain should be up to date, especially those for children and tetanus boosters for adults.
- Courses or boosters of hepatitis A and typhoid vaccines are usually advised.
- Vaccines sometimes recommended are: diphtheria, tuberculosis, rabies, and hepatitis B.
- No certificate of vaccination for yellow fever is required.

OTHER HEALTH CONSIDERATIONS

- Water, food, and personal hygiene advice (including prevention of travellers' diarrhoea)
- Insect bite avoidance (to reduce risk of dengue)
- Avoidance of animal bites (to lessen the risk of rabies)
- Sun and heat precautions
- Accident risks (possibility of carrying a sterile medical pack)
- Risks associated with casual sex and prevention of blood-borne infections
- Full medical insurance

WEATHER – Cancún

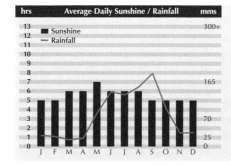

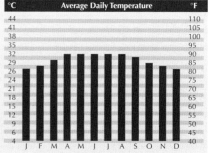

MOLDOVA, REPUBLIC OF

CHIŞINĂU

IMMUNISATION ADVICE

- Immunisations recommended in Britain should be up to date, especially those for children and tetanus boosters for adults.
- Coursed or boosters of hepatitis A and diphtheria vaccines are usually advised.
- Vaccines sometimes recommended are: poliomyelitis, typhoid, tuberculosis, hepatitis B, rabies, and tick-borne encephalitis.
- No certificate of vaccination for yellow fever is required.
- Malaria is not normally present.

OTHER HEALTH CONSIDERATIONS

- Water, food, and personal hygiene advice (including prevention of travellers' diarrhoea)
- Insect bite avoidance
- Avoidance of animal bites (to lessen the risk of rabies)
- Sun and heat precautions (in summer months)
- Accident risks (possibility of carrying a sterile medical pack)
- Risks associated with casual sex and prevention of blood-borne infections
- Full medical insurance

WEATHER – Chisinau

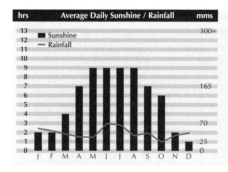

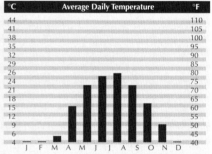

MONGOLIA

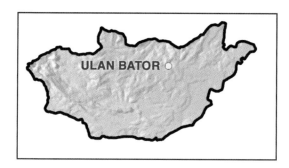

ULAN BATOR ○

IMMUNISATION ADVICE

- Immunisations recommended in Britain should be up to date, especially those for children and tetanus boosters for adults.
- Courses or boosters of hepatitis A, typhoid, and diphtheria vaccines are usually advised.

- Vaccines sometimes recommended are: poliomyelitis, hepatitis B, tuberculosis, meningococcal A and C, and rabies.
- No certificate of vaccination for yellow fever is required.
- Malaria is not normally present.

OTHER HEALTH CONSIDERATIONS

- Water, food, and personal hygiene advice (including prevention of travellers' diarrhoea)
- Insect bite avoidance
- Avoidance of animal bites (to lessen the risk of rabies)
- Sun and heat precautions (in summer months)
- Accident risks (possibility of carrying a sterile medical pack)
- Risks associated with casual sex and prevention of blood-borne infections
- Full medical insurance

WEATHER – Ulan Bator

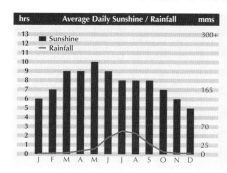

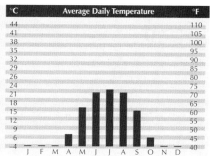

MOROCCO

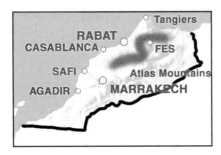

MALARIA ADVICE

- Malaria is a serious and some-times fatal disease transmitted by mosquitoes. There is no vaccine available for malaria.

Malaria Precautions

- The risk of malaria is limited to eastern parts of the country in rural valleys, west of the Atlas mountains (Al Hoceima, Taounate, and Taza provinces), from May to October. Avoid mosquito bites by covering up with clothing (long sleeves and long trousers) especially after sunset, using insect repellents on exposed skin, and, when necessary, sleeping under an impregnated mosquito net.
- Antimalarial tablets are not normally recommended.
- Prompt investigation of fever is essential.

IMMUNISATION ADVICE

- Immunisations recommended in Britain should be up to date, especially those for children and tetanus boosters for adults.
- Courses or boosters of hepatitis A and typhoid vaccines are usually advised.
- Vaccines sometimes recom-mended are: poliomyelitis, diphtheria, hepatitis B, rabies, and tuberculosis.
- No certificate of vaccination for yellow fever is required.

OTHER HEALTH CONSIDERATIONS

- Water, food, and personal hygiene advice (including prevention of travellers' diarrhoea)
- Insect bite avoidance
- Avoidance of animal bites (to lessen the risk of rabies)
- Sun and heat precautions
- Accident risks (possibility of carrying a sterile medical pack)
- Risks associated with casual sex and prevention of blood-borne infections
- Full medical insurance

WEATHER – Marrakech

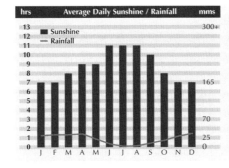

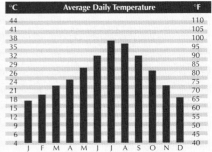

MOZAMBIQUE

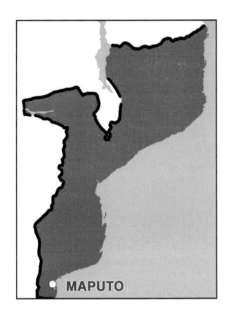

MALARIA ADVICE

- Malaria is a serious and some-times fatal disease transmitted by mosquitoes. There is no vaccine available for malaria.

Malaria Precautions

- Malaria precautions are essential in all areas, all year round. Avoid mosquito bites by covering up with clothing (long sleeves and long trousers) especially after sunset, using insect repellents on exposed skin, and, when necessary, sleeping under an impregnated mosquito net.
- Check with your doctor or nurse about suitable antimalarial tablets.
- Prompt investigation of fever is essential. A person travelling to remote areas should carry, for emergency, standby treatment.

IMMUNISATION ADVICE

- Immunisations recommended in Britain should be up to date, especially those for children and tetanus boosters for adults.
- Courses or boosters of diphtheria, hepatitis A and typhoid vaccines are usually advised.
- Vaccines sometimes recom-mended are: hepatitis B, poliomyelitis, rabies, tuberculosis, and meningococcal A and C.
- A certificate of vaccination for yellow fever is required for anyone over 1 year of age and entering from an infected area.

OTHER HEALTH CONSIDERATIONS

- Water, food, and personal hygiene advice (including prevention of travellers' diarrhoea)
- Insect bite avoidance
- Avoidance of animal bites (to lessen the risk of rabies)
- Other hazards such as bilharzia
- Sun and heat precautions
- Accident risks (possibility of carrying a sterile medical pack)
- Risks associated with casual sex and prevention of blood-borne infections
- Full medical insurance

WEATHER – Maputo

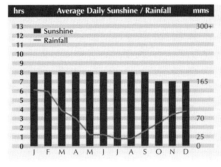

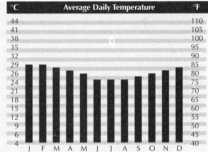

MYANMAR (FORMERLY BURMA)

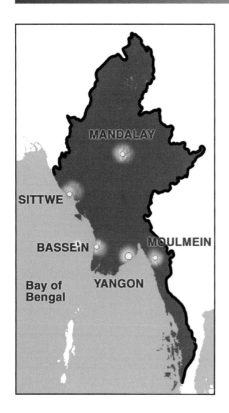

MALARIA ADVICE

- Malaria is a serious and sometimes fatal disease transmitted by mosquitoes. You cannot be vaccinated against malaria.

Malaria Precautions

- Malaria precautions are essential in all areas. Risk is minimal in large cities and there is some seasonal variation in other areas that may need to be taken into account for long-stay travellers.

Avoid mosquito bites by covering up with clothing (long sleeves and long trousers) especially after sunset, using insect repellents on exposed skin, and, when necessary, sleeping under an impregnated mosquito net.
- Check with your doctor or nurse about suitable antimalarial tablets.
- Prompt investigation of fever is essential. A person travelling to remote areas should carry, for emergency, standby treatment.

IMMUNISATION ADVICE

- Immunisations recommended in Britain should be up to date, especially those for children and poliomyelitis and tetanus boosters for adults.
- Courses or boosters of hepatitis A and typhoid vaccines are usually advised.

- Vaccines sometimes recommended are: diphtheria, hepatitis B, rabies, tuberculosis, and Japanese B encephalitis.
- A certificate of vaccination for yellow fever is required if entering from an infected area.

OTHER HEALTH CONSIDERATIONS

- Water, food, and personal hygiene advice (including prevention of travellers' diarrhoea)
- Insect bite avoidance (to reduce risk of dengue)
- Avoidance of animal bites (to lessen the risk of rabies)
- Sun and heat precautions
- Accident risks (possibility of carrying a sterile medical pack)
- Risks associated with casual sex and prevention of blood-borne infections
- Full medical insurance

WEATHER – Mandalay

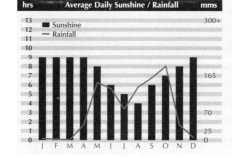

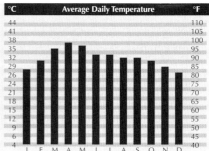

NAMIBIA

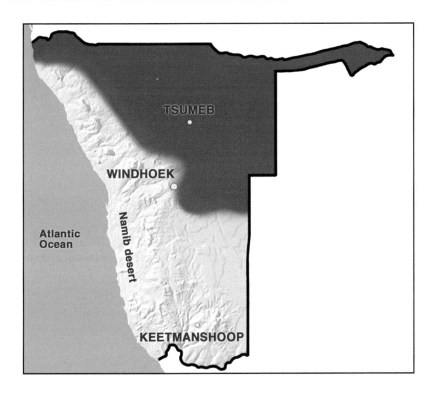

MALARIA ADVICE

- Malaria is a serious and sometimes fatal disease transmitted by mosquitoes. There is no vaccine available for malaria.

Malaria Precautions

- Malaria precautions are essential in the northern third of the country from November to June and along the Kavango and Kunene rivers throughout the year. Avoid mosquito bites by covering up with clothing (long sleeves and long trousers) especially after sunset, using insect repellents on exposed skin, and, when necessary, sleeping under an impregnated mosquito net.
- Check with your doctor or nurse about suitable antimalarial tablets.

- Prompt investigation of fever is essential. A person travelling to remote areas should carry, for emergency, standby treatment.

IMMUNISATION ADVICE

- Immunisations recommended in Britain should be up to date, especially those for children and tetanus boosters for adults.

- Courses or boosters of hepatitis A and typhoid vaccines are usually advised.
- Vaccines sometimes recommended are: diphtheria; hepatitis B, rabies, poliomyelitis, tuberculosis, and meningococcal A and C (mainly in the North).
- A certificate of vaccination for yellow fever is required for anyone entering from an infected area (not if in transit and remaining in main airports and adjacent towns).

OTHER HEALTH CONSIDERATIONS

- Water, food, and personal hygiene advice (including prevention of travellers' diarrhoea)
- Insect bite avoidance
- Avoidance of animal bites (to lessen the risk of rabies)
- Other hazards such as bilharzia
- Sun and heat precautions
- Accident risks (possibility of carrying a sterile medical pack)
- Risks associated with casual sex and prevention of blood-borne infections
- Full medical insurance

WEATHER – Windhoek

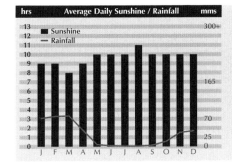

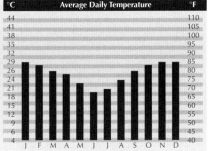

NEPAL

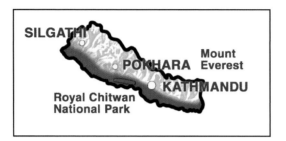

MALARIA ADVICE

- Malaria is a serious and some-times fatal disease transmitted by mosquitoes. There is no vaccine available for malaria.

Malaria Precautions

- Malaria precautions are essential in all areas below 1,300 m, all year round. The risk in Kathmandu and mountainous areas of similar or greater altitude is very small. Avoid mosquito bites by covering up with clothing (long sleeves and long trousers) especially after sunset, using insect repellents on exposed skin, and, when necessary, sleeping under an impregnated mosquito net.
- Check with your doctor or nurse about suitable antimalarial tablets.
- Prompt investigation of fever is essential. A person travelling to remote areas should carry, for emergency, standby treatment.

IMMUNISATION ADVICE

- Immunisations recommended in Britain should be up to date, especially those for children and poliomyelitis and tetanus boosters for adults.
- Courses or boosters of diphtheria, hepatitis A and typhoid vaccines are usually advised.
- Vaccines sometimes recom-mended are: hepatitis B, rabies, tuberculosis, meningococcal A and C, and Japanese B encephalitis (for eastern and low-lying areas).

- A certificate of vaccination for yellow fever is required for anyone entering from an infected area.

OTHER HEALTH CONSIDERATIONS

- Water, food, and personal hygiene advice (including prevention of travellers' diarrhoea)
- Insect bite avoidance (to reduce risk of dengue)
- Avoidance of animal bites (to lessen the risk of rabies)
- Sun and heat precautions
- Accident risks (possibility of carrying a sterile medical pack)
- Risks associated with casual sex and prevention of blood-borne infections
- Full medical insurance

WEATHER – Kathmandu

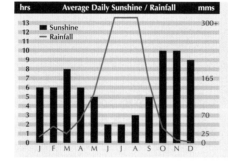

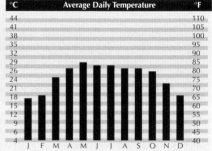

NIGERIA

MALARIA ADVICE

- Malaria is a serious and sometimes fatal disease transmitted by mosquitoes. There is no vaccine available for malaria.

Malaria Precautions

- Malaria precautions are essential in all areas, all year round. Avoid mosquito bites by covering up with clothing (long sleeves and long trousers) especially after sunset, using insect repellents on exposed skin, and, when necessary, sleeping under an impregnated mosquito net.
- Check with your doctor or nurse about suitable antimalarial tablets.
- Prompt investigation of fever is essential. A person travelling to remote areas should carry, for emergency, standby treatment.

IMMUNISATION ADVICE

- Immunisations recommended in Britain should be up to date, especially those for children and poliomyelitis and tetanus boosters for adults.
- Courses or boosters of diphtheria, hepatitis A, typhoid and yellow fever vaccines are usually advised.
- Vaccines sometimes recommended are: diphtheria, tuberculosis, hepatitis B, rabies, and meningococcal A and C (mainly in the North).
- A certificate of vaccination for yellow fever is required for anyone over 1 year of age and entering from an infected area.

OTHER HEALTH CONSIDERATIONS

- Water, food, and personal hygiene advice (including prevention of travellers' diarrhoea)
- Insect bite avoidance (to reduce risk of dengue)
- Avoidance of animal bites (to lessen the risk of rabies)
- Other hazards such as bilharzia
- Sun and heat precautions
- Accident risks (possibility of carrying a sterile medical pack)
- Risks associated with casual sex and prevention of blood-borne infections
- Full medical insurance

WEATHER – Lagos

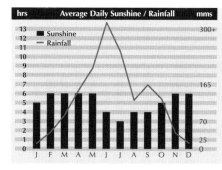

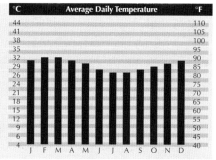

OMAN

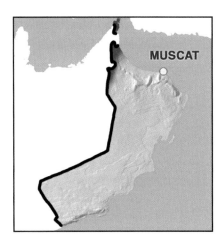

MALARIA ADVICE

- Malaria is a serious and sometimes fatal disease transmitted by mosquitoes. There is no vaccine available for malaria.

Malaria Precautions

- Malaria precautions are essential in limited foci in remote areas in Musandam and North Batinah provinces. Avoid mosquito bites by covering up with clothing (long sleeves and long trousers) especially after sunset, using insect repellents on exposed skin, and, when necessary, sleeping under an impregnated mosquito net.
- Check with your doctor or nurse about suitable antimalarial tablets.

- Prompt investigation of fever is essential. A person travelling to remote areas should carry, for emergency, standby treatment.

IMMUNISATION ADVICE

- Immunisations recommended in Britain should be up to date, especially those for children and tetanus boosters for adults.
- Courses or boosters of hepatitis A and typhoid vaccines are usually advised.
- Vaccine sometimes recommended are: poliomyelitis, tuberculosis, hepatitis B, diphtheria, and rabies.
- A certificate of vaccination for yellow fever is required for anyone entering from an infected area.

OTHER HEALTH CONSIDERATIONS

- Water, food, and personal hygiene advice (including prevention of travellers' diarrhoea)
- Insect bite avoidance
- Avoidance of animal bites (to lessen the risk of rabies)
- Other hazards such as bilharzia
- Sun and heat precautions
- Accident risks
- Risks associated with casual sex and prevention of blood-borne infections
- Full medical insurance

WEATHER – Muscat

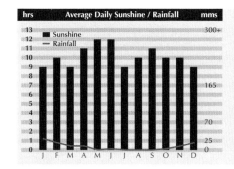

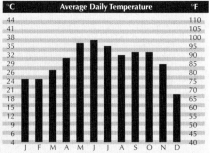

PAKISTAN

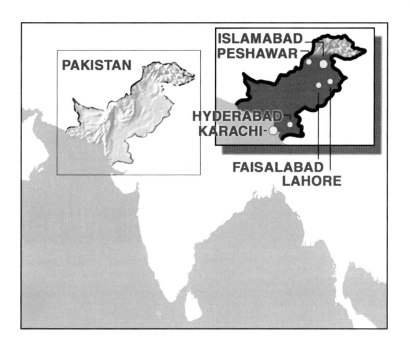

MALARIA ADVICE

- Malaria is a serious and some-times fatal disease transmitted by mosquitoes. There is no vaccine available for malaria.

Malaria Precautions

- Malaria precautions are essential in all areas below 2,000 m, all year round. Avoid mosquito bites by covering up with clothing (long sleeves and long trousers) especially after sunset, using insect repellents on exposed skin, and, when necessary, sleeping under an impregnated mosquito net.
- Check with your doctor or nurse about suitable antimalarials.
- Prompt investigation of fever is essential. A person travelling to remote areas should carry, for emergency, standby treatment.

IMMUNISATION ADVICE

- Immunisations recommended in Britain should be up to date, especially those for children and poliomyelitis and tetanus boosters for adults.
- Courses or boosters of diphtheria, hepatitis A and typhoid vaccines are usually advised.
- Vaccines sometimes recommended are: tuberculosis, hepatitis B, and rabies.
- A certificate of vaccination for yellow fever is required for anyone over 6 months old and entering from an infected area.

OTHER HEALTH CONSIDERATIONS

- Water, food, and personal hygiene advice (including prevention of travellers' diarrhoea)
- Insect bite avoidance (to reduce risk of dengue)
- Avoidance of animal bites (to lessen the risk of rabies)
- Sun and heat precautions
- Accident risks (possibility of carrying a sterile medical pack)
- Risks associated with casual sex and prevention of blood-borne infections
- Full medical insurance

WEATHER – Karachi

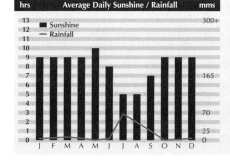

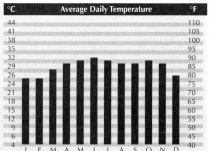

PANAMA

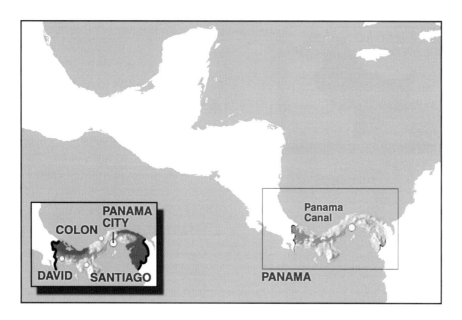

MALARIA ADVICE

- Malaria is a serious and some-times fatal disease transmitted by mosquitoes. There is no vaccine available for malaria.

Malaria Precautions

- Malaria precautions are essential in Bacas de Toro in the west and Darien and San Blas in the east, all year round. Risk is small for those passing through the canal. Avoid mosquito bites by covering up with clothing (long sleeves and long trousers) especially after sunset, using insect repellents on exposed skin, and, when necessary, sleeping under an impregnated mosquito net.
- Check with your doctor or nurse about suitable antimalarial tablets.
- Prompt investigation of fever is essential. A person travelling to remote areas should carry, for emergency, standby treatment.

IMMUNISATION ADVICE

- Immunisations recommended in Britain should be up to date, especially those for children and tetanus boosters for adults.
- Courses or boosters of hepatitis A, typhoid, and yellow fever vaccines are usually advised.

- Vaccines sometimes recom-mended are: diphtheria, tuberculosis, rabies, and hepatitis B.
- A certificate of vaccination for yellow fever is recommended for all travellers going to Chepo, Darien and San Blas.

OTHER HEALTH CONSIDERATIONS

- Water, food, and personal hygiene advice (including prevention of travellers' diarrhoea)
- Insect bite avoidance (to reduce risk of dengue)
- Avoidance of animal bites (to lessen the risk of rabies)
- Sun and heat precautions
- Accident risks (possibility of carrying a sterile medical pack)
- Risks associated with casual sex and prevention of blood-borne infections
- Full medical insurance

WEATHER – Panama City

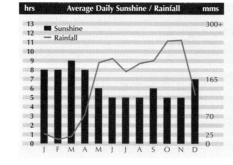

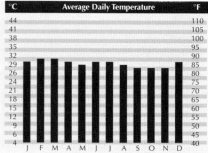

PAPUA NEW GUINEA

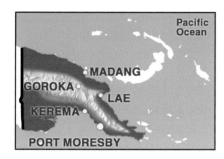

MALARIA ADVICE

- Malaria is a serious and some-times fatal disease transmitted by mosquitoes. There is no vaccine available for malaria.

Malaria Precautions

- Malaria precautions are essential in all areas below 1,800 m, all year round. Avoid mosquito bites by covering up with clothing (long sleeves and long trousers) especially after sunset, using insect repellents on exposed skin, and, when necessary, sleeping under an impregnated mosquito net.
- Check with your doctor or nurse about suitable antimalarial tablets.

- Prompt investigation of fever is essential. A person travelling to remote areas should carry, for emergency, standby treatment.

IMMUNISATION ADVICE

- Immunisations recommended in Britain should be up to date, especially those for children and tetanus boosters for adults.
- Courses or boosters of hepatitis A and typhoid vaccines are usually advised.
- Vaccines sometimes recommended are: diphtheria, tuberculosis, hepatitis B, and poliomyelitis.
- A certificate of vaccination for yellow fever is required for anyone over 1 year of age and entering from an infected area.

OTHER HEALTH CONSIDERATIONS

- Water, food, and personal hygiene advice (including prevention of travellers' diarrhoea)
- Insect bite avoidance (to reduce risk of dengue)
- Avoidance of animal bites
- Sun and heat precautions
- Accident risks (possibility of carrying a sterile medical pack)
- Risks associated with casual sex and prevention of blood-borne infections
- Full medical insurance

WEATHER – Port Moresby

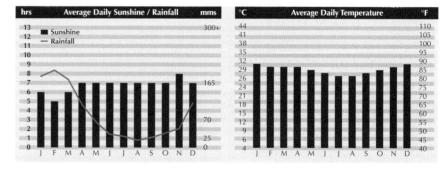

PERU

MALARIA ADVICE

- Malaria is a serious and sometimes fatal disease transmitted by mosquitoes. There is no vaccine available for malaria.

Malaria Precautions

- Malaria precautions are essential in low-lying rural areas all year round. Risk is minimal west of the Andes. Avoid mosquito bites by covering up with clothing (long sleeves and long trousers) especially after sunset, using insect repellents on exposed skin, and, when necessary, sleeping under an impregnated mosquito net.
- Check with your doctor or nurse about suitable antimalarial tablets.

- Prompt investigation of fever is essential. A person travelling to remote areas should carry, for emergency, standby treatment.

IMMUNISATION ADVICE

- Immunisations recommended in Britain should be up to date, especially those for children and tetanus boosters for adults.

- Courses or boosters of hepatitis A, typhoid, and yellow fever vaccines (for those visiting rural/jungle areas below 2,300 m) are usually advised.
- Vaccines sometimes recommended are: diphtheria, tuberculosis, rabies, and hepatitis B.
- A certificate of vaccination for yellow fever is required for anyone over 6 months of age and entering from an infected area.

OTHER HEALTH CONSIDERATIONS

- Water, food, and personal hygiene advice (including prevention of travellers' diarrhoea)
- Insect bite avoidance
- Avoidance of animal bites (to lessen the risk of rabies)
- Sun and heat precautions
- Accident risks (possibility of carrying a sterile medical pack)
- Risks associated with casual sex and prevention of blood-borne infections
- Full medical insurance

WEATHER – Lima

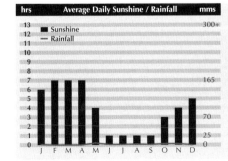

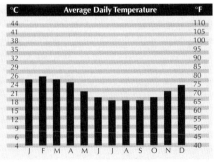

PHILIPPINES

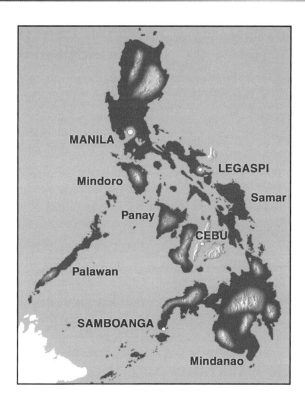

MALARIA ADVICE

- Malaria is a serious and some-times fatal disease transmitted by mosquitoes. There is no vaccine available for malaria.

Malaria Precautions

- Malaria precautions are essential in all areas below 600 m (except in the provinces of Bohol, Catanduanes, Cebu, and Leyte) all year round. Risk is minimal in urban areas and the plains all year round. Avoid mosquito bites by covering up with clothing (long sleeves and long trousers) especially after sunset, using insect repellents on exposed skin, and, when necessary, sleeping under an impregnated mosquito net.

- Check with your doctor or nurse about suitable antimalarial tablets.
- Prompt investigation of fever is essential. A person travelling to remote areas should carry, for emergency, standby treatment.

IMMUNISATION ADVICE

- Immunisations recommended in Britain should be up to date,

especially those for children and tetanus boosters for adults.
- Courses or boosters of diphtheria, hepatitis A and typhoid vaccines are usually advised.
- Vaccines sometimes recom-mended are: tuberculosis, hepatitis B, rabies, Japanese B encephalitis, and poliomyelitis.
- A certificate of vaccination for yellow fever is required for anyone over 1 year of age and entering from an infected area.

OTHER HEALTH CONSIDERATIONS

- Water, food, and personal hygiene advice (including prevention of travellers' diarrhoea)
- Insect bite avoidance (to reduce risk of dengue)
- Avoidance of animal bites (to lessen the risk of rabies)
- Other hazards such as bilharzia
- Sun and heat precautions
- Accident risks (possibility of carrying a sterile medical pack)
- Risks associated with casual sex and prevention of blood-borne infections
- Full medical insurance

WEATHER – Manila

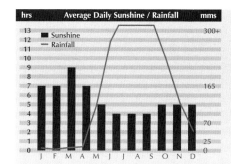

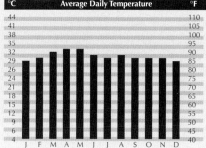

POLAND

IMMUNISATION ADVICE

- Immunisations recommended in Britain should be up to date, especially those for children and tetanus boosters for adults.
- Vaccines sometimes recommended are: poliomyelitis, hepatitis A, tick-borne encephalitis, rabies, typhoid, hepatitis B, diphtheria, and tuberculosis.
- No certificate of vaccination for yellow fever is required.
- Malaria is not normally present.

OTHER HEALTH CONSIDERATIONS

- Water, food, and personal hygiene advice (including prevention of travellers' diarrhoea)
- Insect bite avoidance
- Avoidance of animal bites (to lessen the risk of rabies)
- Sun and heat precautions (in summer months)
- Accident risks (possibility of carrying a sterile medical pack)
- Risks associated with casual sex and prevention of blood-borne infections
- Full medical insurance

WEATHER – Warsaw

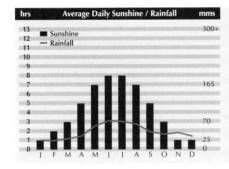

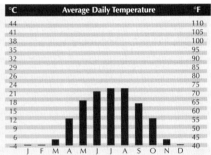

PUERTO RICO

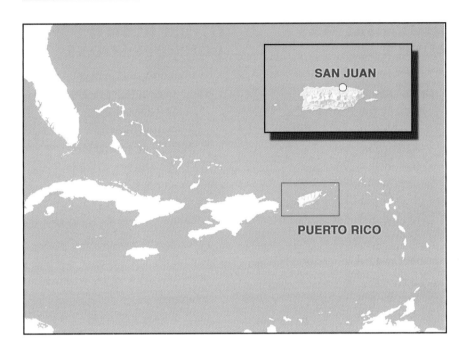

SAN JUAN

PUERTO RICO

OTHER HEALTH CONSIDERATIONS

- Water, food, and personal hygiene advice (including prevention of travellers' diarrhoea)
- Insect bite avoidance (to reduce risk of dengue)
- Avoidance of animal bites (to lessen the risk of rabies)
- Other hazards such as bilharzia
- Sun and heat precautions
- Accident risks (possibility of carrying a sterile medical pack)
- Risks associated with casual sex and prevention of blood-borne infections
- Full medical insurance

IMMUNISATION ADVICE

- Immunisations recommended in Britain should be up to date, especially those for children and tetanus boosters for adults.
- Courses or boosters of hepatitis A and typhoid vaccines are usually advised.
- Vaccines sometimes recommended are: diphtheria, tuberculosis, rabies, and hepatitis B.
- No certificate of vaccination for yellow fever is required.
- Malaria is not normally present.

WEATHER – San Juan

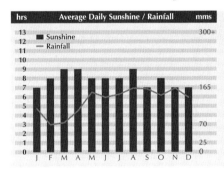

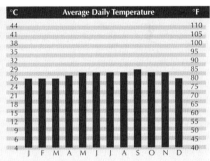

ROMANIA

IMMUNISATION ADVICE

- Immunisations recommended in Britain should be up to date, especially those for children and tetanus boosters for adults.
- Courses or boosters of hepatitis A and diphtheria vaccines are usually advised.
- Vaccines sometimes recommended are: poliomyelitis, typhoid, tuberculosis, hepatitis B, rabies, and tick-borne encephalitis.
- No certificate of vaccination for yellow fever is required.
- Malaria is not normally present.

OTHER HEALTH CONSIDERATIONS

- Water, food, and personal hygiene advice (including prevention of travellers' diarrhoea)
- Insect bite avoidance
- Avoidance of animal bites (to lessen the risk of rabies)
- Sun and heat precautions (in summer months)
- Accident risks (possibility of carrying a sterile medical pack)
- Risks associated with casual sex and prevention of blood-borne infections
- Full medical insurance

WEATHER – Bucharest

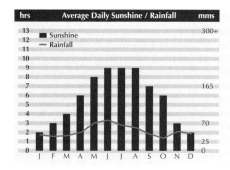

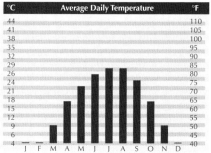

RUSSIAN FEDERATION

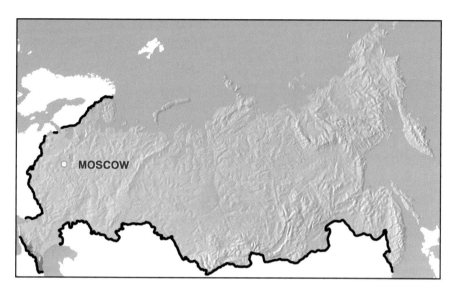

MOSCOW

OTHER HEALTH CONSIDERATIONS

- Water, food, and personal hygiene advice (including prevention of travellers' diarrhoea)
- Insect bite avoidance
- Avoidance of animal bites (to lessen the risk of rabies)
- Sun and heat precautions (in summer months)
- Accident risks (possibility of carrying a sterile medical pack)
- Risks associated with casual sex and prevention of blood-borne infections
- Full medical insurance

IMMUNISATION ADVICE

- Immunisations recommended in Britain should be up to date, especially those for children and tetanus boosters for adults.
- Courses or boosters of hepatitis A, diphtheria, and typhoid vaccines (for areas east of the Ural mountains) are usually advised.
- Vaccines sometimes recommended are: poliomyelitis, typhoid, tuberculosis, hepatitis B, rabies, tick-borne encephalitis, and Japanese B encephalitis (only in the very far east of Siberia close to China).

- No certificate of vaccination for yellow fever is required.
- Malaria is not normally present.

WEATHER – Moscow

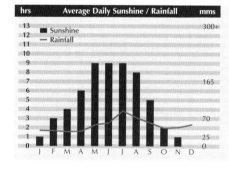

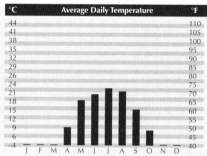

SAINT KITTS AND NEVIS

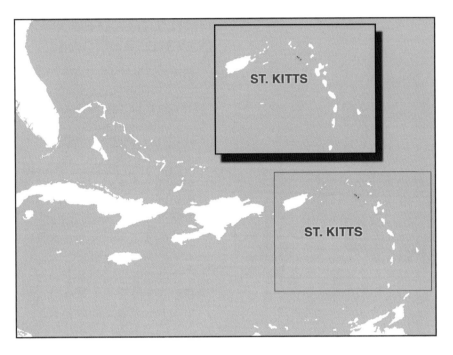

OTHER HEALTH CONSIDERATIONS

- Water, food, and personal hygiene advice (including prevention of travellers' diarrhoea)
- Insect bite avoidance (to reduce risk of dengue)
- Avoidance of animal bites
- Sun and heat precautions
- Accident risks (possibility of carrying a sterile medical pack)
- Risks associated with casual sex and prevention of blood-borne infections
- Full medical insurance

IMMUNISATION ADVICE

- Immunisations recommended in Britain should be up to date, especially those for children and tetanus boosters for adults.
- A course or booster of hepatitis A vaccine is usually advised.
- Vaccines sometimes recommended are: typhoid, diphtheria, hepatitis B, and tuberculosis.
- A certificate of vaccination for yellow fever is required for anyone over 1 year of age and entering from an infected area.
- Malaria is not normally present.

WEATHER – St. Kitts

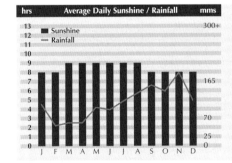

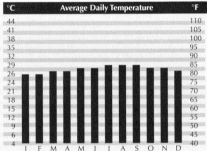

SAINT LUCIA

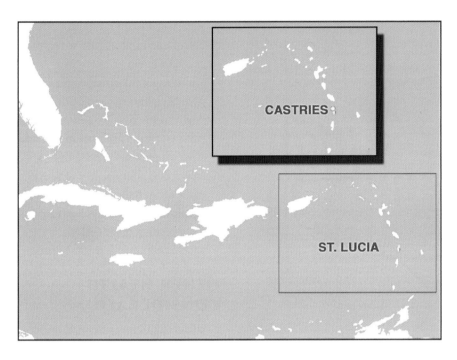

OTHER HEALTH CONSIDERATIONS

- Water, food, and personal hygiene advice (including prevention of travellers' diarrhoea)
- Insect bite avoidance (to reduce risk of dengue)
- Avoidance of animal bites
- Sun and heat precautions
- Accident risks (possibility of carrying a sterile medical pack)
- Risks associated with casual sex and prevention of blood-borne infections
- Full medical insurance

IMMUNISATION ADVICE

- Immunisations recommended in Britain should be up to date, especially those for children and tetanus boosters for adults.
- A course or booster of hepatitis A vaccine is usually advised.
- Vaccines sometimes recommended are: typhoid, diphtheria, hepatitis B, and tuberculosis.
- A certificate of vaccination for yellow fever is required for anyone over 1 year of age and entering from an infected area.
- Malaria is not normally present.

WEATHER – Castries

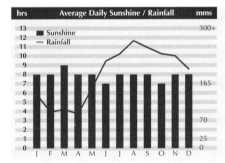

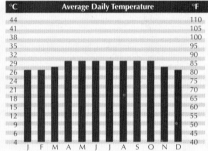

SAUDI ARABIA

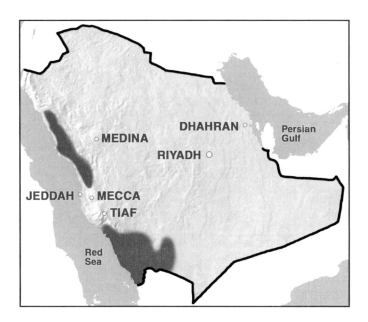

MALARIA ADVICE

- Malaria is a serious and sometimes fatal disease transmitted by mosquitoes. There is no vaccine available for malaria.

Malaria Precautions

- Malaria precautions are essential only in the southwest province (the eastern, northern and central provinces, mountainous areas, Jeddah, Mecca, Medina, and Taif are usually malaria free) all year round. Avoid mosquito bites by covering up with clothing (long sleeves and long trousers) especially after sunset, using insect repellents on exposed skin, and, when necessary, sleeping under an impregnated mosquito net.
- Check with your doctor or nurse about suitable antimalarial tablets.
- Prompt investigation of fever is essential. A person travelling to remote areas should carry, for emergency, standby treatment.

IMMUNISATION ADVICE

- Immunisations recommended in Britain should be up to date, especially those for children and tetanus boosters for adults.
- A course or booster of hepatitis A vaccine is usually advised.
- Vaccines sometimes recommended are: poliomyelitis, typhoid, tuberculosis, diphtheria, hepatitis B, rabies, and meningococcal ACWY.
- A certificate of vaccination for yellow fever is required for anyone entering from an infected area.

- A certificate of vaccination for meningococcal ACWY is required as a condition of entry if attending a pilgrimage and from ALL travellers arriving from the "meningitis belt" of sub-Saharan Africa. Details are normally made clear when visas are requested and certificates are not required from other categories of visitors or expatriate workers. Certificates are considered valid 10 days after vaccination and last for 3 years.

OTHER HEALTH CONSIDERATIONS

- Water, food, and personal hygiene advice (including prevention of travellers' diarrhoea)
- Insect bite avoidance (to reduce risk of dengue)
- Avoidance of animal bites (to lessen the risk of rabies)
- Other hazards such as bilharzia
- Sun and heat precautions
- Accident risks (possibility of carrying a sterile medical pack)
- Risks associated with casual sex and prevention of blood-borne infections
- Full medical insurance

WEATHER – Riyadh

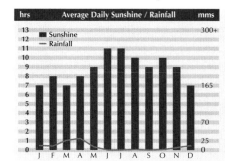

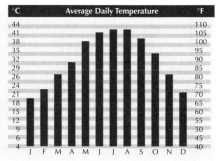

SERBIA/MONTENEGRO

IMMUNISATION ADVICE

- Immunisations recommended in Britain should be up to date, especially those for children and tetanus boosters for adults.
- A course or booster of hepatitis A vaccine is usually advised.
- Vaccines sometimes recommended are: poliomyelitis, typhoid, tuberculosis, hepatitis B, diphtheria, rabies, and tick-borne encephalitis.
- No certificate of vaccination for yellow fever is required.
- Malaria is not normally present.

OTHER HEALTH CONSIDERATIONS

- Water, food, and personal hygiene advice (including prevention of travellers' diarrhoea)
- Insect bite avoidance
- Avoidance of animal bites (to lessen the risk of rabies)
- Sun and heat precautions (in summer months)
- Accident risks (possibility of carrying a sterile medical pack)
- Risks associated with casual sex and prevention of blood-borne infections
- Full medical insurance

WEATHER – Belgrade

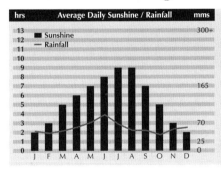

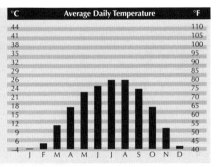

SEYCHELLES

MAHÉ

MADAGASCAR

IMMUNISATION ADVICE

- Immunisations recommended in Britain should be up to date, especially those for children and tetanus boosters for adults.
- Courses or boosters of diphtheria, hepatitis A and typhoid vaccines are usually advised.
- Vaccines sometimes recommended are: poliomyelitis, tuberculosis, hepatitis B, and rabies.

- A certificate of vaccination for yellow fever is required for anyone over 1 year of age and entering from an infected area within the preceding 6 days.
- Malaria is not normally present.

OTHER HEALTH CONSIDERATIONS

- Water, food, and personal hygiene advice (including prevention of travellers' diarrhoea)

- Insect bite avoidance
- Avoidance of animal bites (to lessen the risk of rabies)
- Sun and heat precautions
- Accident risks (possibility of carrying a sterile medical pack)
- Risks associated with casual sex and prevention of blood-borne infections
- Full medical insurance

WEATHER – Mahé

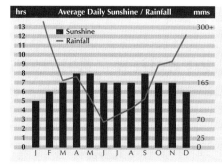

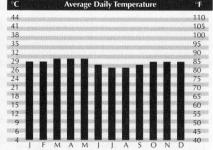

SINGAPORE

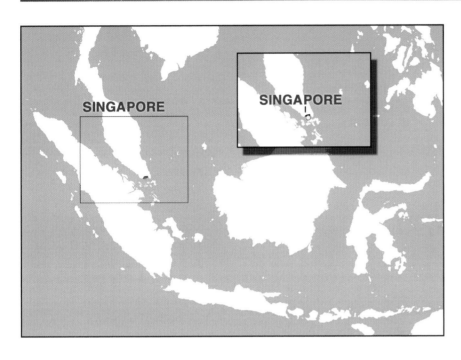

OTHER HEALTH CONSIDERATIONS

- Water, food, and personal hygiene advice (including prevention of travellers' diarrhoea)
- Insect bite avoidance (to reduce risk of dengue)
- Avoidance of animal bites (to lessen the risk of rabies)
- Sun and heat precautions
- Accident risks
- Risks associated with casual sex and prevention of blood-borne infections
- Full medical insurance

IMMUNISATION ADVICE

- Immunisations recommended in Britain should be up to date, especially those for children.
- Vaccines sometimes recommended are: hepatitis A, typhoid, diphtheria, hepatitis B, tuberculosis, and poliomyelitis.
- Rabies is present, but postexposure treatment should be readily available.
- A certificate of vaccination for yellow fever is required for anyone over 1 year of age and entering from an infected area.
- Malaria is not normally present.

WEATHER – Singapore

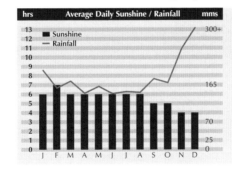

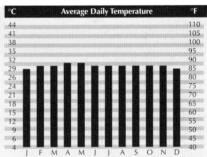

SLOVAKIA

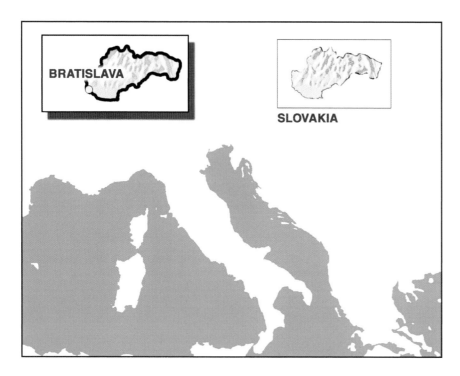

BRATISLAVA

SLOVAKIA

OTHER HEALTH CONSIDERATIONS

- Water, food, and personal hygiene advice (including prevention of travellers' diarrhoea)
- Insect bite avoidance
- Avoidance of animal bites (to lessen the risk of rabies)
- Sun and heat precautions (in summer months)
- Accident risks (possibility of carrying a sterile medical pack)
- Risks associated with casual sex and prevention of blood-borne infections
- Full medical insurance

IMMUNISATION ADVICE

- Immunisations recommended in Britain should be up to date, especially those for children and tetanus boosters for adults.
- Vaccines sometimes recommended are: poliomyelitis, hepatitis A, typhoid, diphtheria, tick-borne encephalitis, and hepatitis B.
- Rabies is present, but postexposure treatment should be readily available.
- No certificate of vaccination for yellow fever is required.
- Malaria is not normally present.

WEATHER – Bratislava

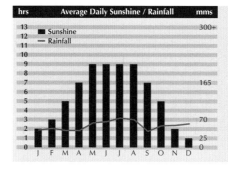

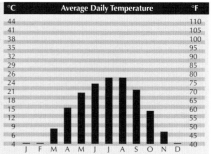

SLOVENIA

OTHER HEALTH CONSIDERATIONS

- Water, food, and personal hygiene advice (including prevention of travellers' diarrhoea)
- Insect bite avoidance
- Avoidance of animal bites (to lessen the risk of rabies)

- Sun and heat precautions (in summer months)
- Accident risks (possibility of carrying a sterile medical pack)
- Risks associated with casual sex and prevention of blood-borne infections
- Full medical insurance

IMMUNISATION ADVICE

- Immunisations recommended in Britain should be up to date, especially those for children and tetanus boosters for adults.
- A course or booster of hepatitis A vaccine is usually advised.
- Vaccines sometimes recommended are: poliomyelitis, typhoid, rabies, hepatitis B, diphtheria, tuberculosis, and tick-borne encephalitis.
- No certificate of vaccination for yellow fever is required.
- Malaria is not normally present.

WEATHER – Ljubljana

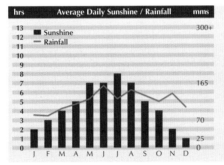

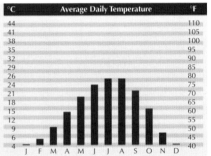

SOUTH AFRICA

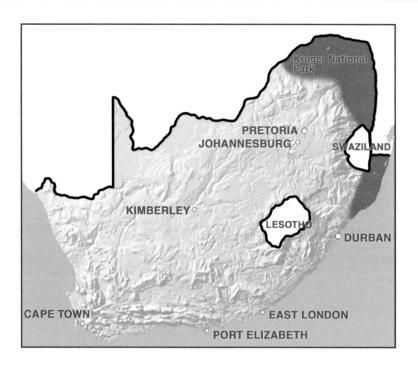

MALARIA ADVICE

- Malaria is a serious and some-times fatal disease transmitted by mosquitoes. There is no vaccine available for malaria.

Malaria Precautions

- Malaria precautions are essential in the low-altitude areas of Mpumalanga province (including Kruger National Park), Northern province, and northeastern KwaZulu-Natal as far south as the Tugela river, all year round. Risk is highest from October to May. The rest of the country is normally malaria free. Avoid mosquito bites by covering up with clothing (long sleeves and long trousers) especially after sunset, using insect repellents on exposed skin, and, when necessary, sleeping under an impregnated mosquito net.

- Check with your doctor or nurse about suitable antimalarial tablets
- Prompt investigation of fever is essential. A person travelling to remote areas should carry, for emergency, standby treatment.

IMMUNISATION ADVICE

- Immunisations recommended in Britain should be up to date, especially those for children and tetanus boosters for adults.
- Courses or boosters of hepatitis A and typhoid vaccines are usually advised.
- Vaccines sometimes recom-mended are: tuberculosis, hepatitis B, rabies, poliomyelitis, and diphtheria.
- A certificate of vaccination for yellow fever is required for anyone over 1 year of age and entering from an infected area.

OTHER HEALTH CONSIDERATIONS

- Water, food, and personal hygiene advice (including prevention of travellers' diarrhoea)
- Insect bite avoidance
- Avoidance of animal bites (to lessen the risk of rabies)
- Other hazards such as bilharzia
- Sun and heat precautions
- Accident risks (possibility of carrying a sterile medical pack)
- Risks associated with casual sex and prevention of blood-borne infections
- Full medical insurance

WEATHER – Durban

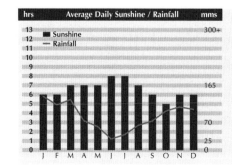

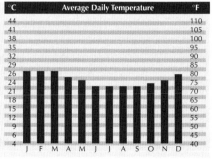

SRI LANKA

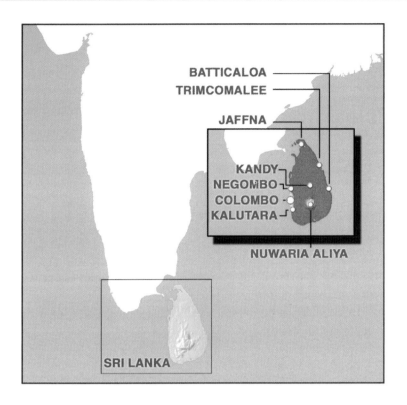

MALARIA ADVICE

- Malaria is a serious and some-times fatal disease transmitted by mosquitoes. There is no vaccine available for malaria.

Malaria Precautions

- Malaria precautions are essential in the whole country (except for the districts of Colombo, Kalutra, and Nuwara Eliya) all year round. Avoid mosquito bites by covering up with clothing (long sleeves and long trousers) especially after sunset, using insect repellents on exposed skin, and, when necessary, sleeping under an impregnated mosquito net.
- Check with your doctor or nurse about suitable antimalarial tablets.

- Prompt investigation of fever is essential. A person travelling to remote areas should carry, for emergency, standby treatment.

IMMUNISATION ADVICE

- Immunisations recommended in Britain should be up to date, especially those for children and tetanus boosters for adults.
- Courses or boosters of hepatitis A and typhoid vaccines are usually advised.
- Vaccines sometimes recommended are: tuberculosis, hepatitis B, rabies, poliomyelitis, diphtheria, and Japanese B encephalitis.
- A certificate of vaccination for yellow fever is required for anyone over 1 year of age and entering from an infected area.

OTHER HEALTH CONSIDERATIONS

- Water, food, and personal hygiene advice (including prevention of travellers' diarrhoea)
- Insect bite avoidance (to reduce risk of dengue)
- Avoidance of animal bites (to lessen the risk of rabies)
- Sun and heat precautions
- Accident risks (possibility of carrying a sterile medical pack)
- Risks associated with casual sex and prevention of blood-borne infections
- Full medical insurance

WEATHER – Colombo

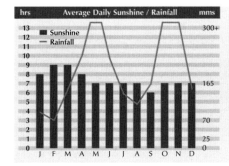

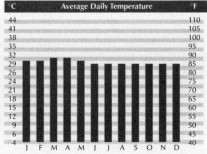

TAJIKISTAN

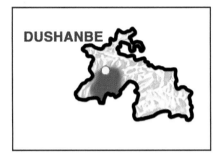

MALARIA ADVICE

- Malaria is a serious and some-times fatal disease transmitted by mosquitoes. There is no vaccine available for malaria.

Malaria Precautions

- Malaria precautions are essential particularly in southern border areas (Khatlon region), and in some central (Dushanbe), western (Gorno-Badakhshan), and northern (Leninabad) areas from June to October. Avoid mosquito bites by covering up with clothing (long sleeves and long trousers) especially after sunset, using insect repellents on exposed skin, and when necessary, sleeping under an impregnated mosquito net

- Check with your doctor or nurse about suitable antimalarials.
- Prompt investigation of fever is essential.

IMMUNISATION ADVICE

- Immunisations recommended in Britain should be up to date, especially those for children and tetanus boosters for adults.
- Courses or boosters of hepatitis A, typhoid and diphtheria vaccines are usually advised.
- Vaccines sometimes recommended are: tuberculosis, rabies, hepatitis B, poliomyelitis, and tick-borne encephalitis.
- No certificate of vaccination for yellow fever is required.

OTHER HEALTH CONSIDERATIONS

- Water, food, and personal hygiene advice (including prevention of travellers' diarrhoea)
- Insect bite avoidance
- Avoidance of animal bites (to lessen the risk of rabies)
- Sun and heat precautions (in summer months)
- Accident risks (possibility of carrying a sterile medical pack)
- Risks associated with casual sex and prevention of blood-borne infections
- Full medical insurance

WEATHER – Dushanbe

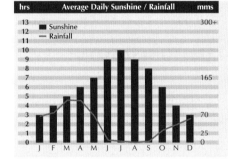

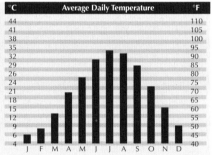

THAILAND

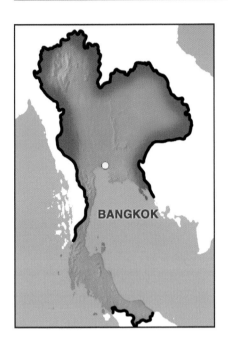

BANGKOK

MALARIA ADVICE

- Malaria is a serious and some-times fatal disease transmitted by mosquitoes. There is no vaccine available for malaria.

Malaria Precautions

- Malaria precautions are essential in Ko Chang and along the borders of Laos, Cambodia, and Myanmar, all year round. (There is very little risk in cities and main tourist areas such as Phuket, Pattaya, Bangkok, Changmai, the river Quai bridge area, and offshore islands except Ko Chang.) Avoid mosquito bites by covering up with clothing (long sleeves and long trousers) especially after sunset, using insect repellents on exposed skin, and, when necessary, sleeping under an impregnated mosquito net.
- Check with your doctor or nurse about suitable antimalarial tablets.
- Prompt investigation of fever is essential. A person travelling to remote areas should carry, for emergency, standby treatment.

IMMUNISATION ADVICE

- Immunisations recommended in Britain should be up to date, especially those for children and tetanus boosters for adults.
- Courses or boosters of diphtheria, hepatitis A and typhoid vaccines are usually advised.
- Vaccines sometimes recommended are: tuberculosis, rabies, poliomyelitis, Japanese B encephalitis, and hepatitis B.
- A certificate of vaccination for yellow fever is required for anyone over 1 year of age and entering from an infected area.

OTHER HEALTH CONSIDERATIONS

- Water, food, and personal hygiene advice (including prevention of travellers' diarrhoea)
- Insect bite avoidance (to reduce risk of dengue)
- Avoidance of animal bites (to lessen the risk of rabies)
- Sun and heat precautions
- Accident risks (possibility of carrying a sterile medical pack)
- Risks associated with casual sex and prevention of blood-borne infections
- Full medical insurance

WEATHER – Bangkok

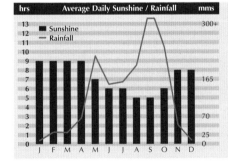

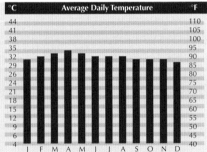

TRINIDAD AND TOBAGO

IMMUNISATION ADVICE

- Immunisations recommended in Britain should be up to date, especially those for children and tetanus boosters for adults.
- A course or booster of hepatitis A vaccine is usually advised.
- Vaccines sometimes recommended are: diphtheria, typhoid, hepatitis B, tuberculosis, rabies, and yellow fever.
- Although no human cases have been recorded, the yellow fever virus is present in monkeys on the islands. Mosquitos who have bitten these monkeys are then a possible risk to humans. Travellers likely to be close to the monkeys (eg, in rural areas), should be immunized.

- A certificate of vaccination for yellow fever is required for anyone over 1 year of age and entering from an infected area.
- Malaria is not normally present.

OTHER HEALTH CONSIDERATIONS

- Water, food, and personal hygiene advice (including prevention of travellers' diarrhoea)
- Insect bite avoidance (to reduce risk of dengue)
- Avoidance of animal bites (to lessen the risk of rabies)
- Sun and heat precautions
- Accident risks (possibility of carrying a sterile medical pack)
- Risks associated with casual sex and prevention of blood-borne infections
- Full medical insurance

WEATHER – Trinidad

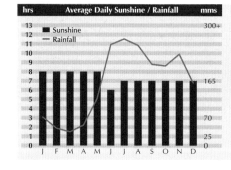
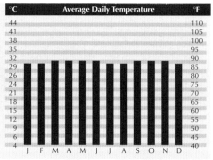

TUNISIA

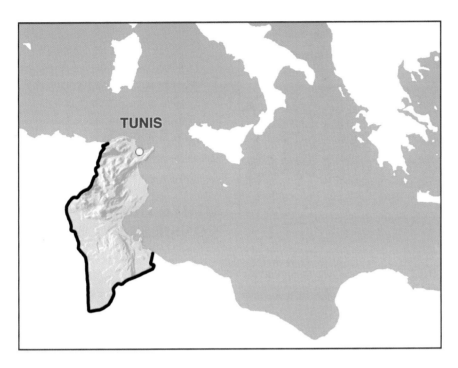

TUNIS

OTHER HEALTH CONSIDERATIONS

- Water, food, and personal hygiene advice (including prevention of travellers' diarrhoea)
- Insect bite avoidance
- Avoidance of animal bites (to lessen the risk of rabies)
- Sun and heat precautions
- Accident risks (possibility of carrying a sterile medical pack)
- Risks associated with casual sex and prevention of blood-borne infections
- Full medical insurance

IMMUNISATION ADVICE

- Immunisations recommended in Britain should be up to date, especially those for children and tetanus boosters for adults.
- Courses or boosters of hepatitis A and typhoid vaccines are usually advised.
- Vaccines sometimes recommended are: poliomyelitis, diphtheria, hepatitis B, tuberculosis, and rabies.
- A certificate of vaccination for yellow fever is required for anyone over 1 year of age and entering from an infected area.
- Malaria is not normally present.

WEATHER – Tunis

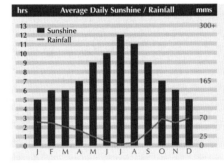

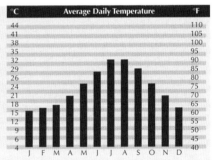

TURKEY

MALARIA ADVICE

- Malaria is a serious and sometimes fatal disease transmitted by mosquitoes. There is no vaccine available for malaria.

MALARIA PRECAUTIONS

- Malaria precautions are essential only in the far eastern provinces of Cukurova, Amikova, and the low-lying areas around Side and Adana in coastal Anatolia, from May to October. (There is minimal or no malarial risk in the main tourist areas in the west and southwest of the country.) Avoid mosquito bites by covering up with clothing (long sleeves and long trousers) especially after sunset, using insect repellents on exposed skin, and, when necessary, sleeping under an impregnated mosquito net.

- Check with your doctor or nurse about suitable antimalarial tablets.
- Prompt investigation of fever is essential.

IMMUNISATION ADVICE

- Immunisations recommended in Britain should be up to date, especially those for children and tetanus boosters for adults.

- Courses or boosters of diphtheria, hepatitis A vaccines are usually advised.
- Vaccines sometimes recommended are: tuberculosis, hepatitis B, rabies, poliomyelitis, and typhoid.
- No certificate of vaccination for yellow fever is required.

OTHER HEALTH CONSIDERATIONS

- Water, food, and personal hygiene advice (including prevention of travellers' diarrhoea)
- Insect bite avoidance
- Avoidance of animal bites (to lessen the risk of rabies)
- Sun and heat precautions
- Accident risks (possibility of carrying a sterile medical pack)
- Risks associated with casual sex and prevention of blood-borne infections
- Full medical insurance

WEATHER – Istanbul

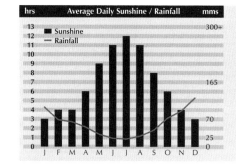

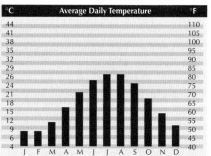

TURKMENISTAN

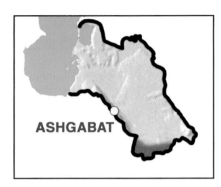

ASHGABAT

MALARIA ADVICE

- Malaria is a serious and sometimes fatal disease transmitted by mosquitos. There is no vaccine available for malaria.

Malaria Precautions

- Malaria precautions are essential in the southeast, mainly Mary district, from June to October. Avoid mosquito bites by covering up with clothing (long sleeves and long trousers) especially after sunset, using insect repellents on exposed skin, and, when necessary, sleeping under an impregnated mosquito net.
- Check with your doctor or nurse about suitable antimalarial tablets.
- Prompt investigation of a fever is essential.

IMMUNISATION ADVICE

- Immunisations recommended in Britain should be up to date, especially those for children and tetanus boosters for adults.
- Courses or boosters of diphtheria, hepatitis A and typhoid vaccines are usually advised.
- Vaccines sometimes recommended are: tuberculosis, hepatitis B, rabies, poliomyelitis, and tick-borne encephalitis.
- No certificate of vaccination for yellow fever is required.

OTHER HEALTH CONSIDERATIONS

- Water, food, and personal hygiene advice (including prevention of travellers' diarrhoea)
- Insect bite avoidance
- Avoidance of animal bites (to lessen the risk of rabies)
- Sun and heat precautions
- Accident risks (possibility of carrying a sterile medical pack)
- Risks associated with casual sex and prevention of blood-borne infections
- Full medical insurance

WEATHER – Ashgabat

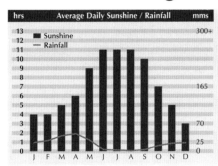

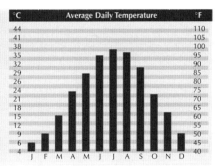

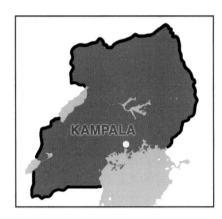

MALARIA ADVICE

• Malaria is a serious and some-times fatal disease transmitted by mosquitoes. There is no vaccine available for malaria.

Malaria Precautions

• Malaria precautions are essential in all areas all year round. Avoid mosquito bites by covering up with clothing (long sleeves and long trousers) especially after sunset, using insect repellents on exposed skin, and, when necessary, sleeping under an impregnated mosquito net.
• Check with your doctor or nurse about suitable antimalarial tablets.
• Prompt investigation of fever is essential. A person travelling to remote areas should carry, for emergency, standby treatment.

IMMUNISATION ADVICE

• Immunisations recommended in Britain should be up to date, especially those for children and tetanus boosters for adults.
• Courses or boosters of diphtheria, hepatitis A, typhoid and yellow fever vaccines are usually advised.
• Vaccines sometimes recommended are: tuberculosis, hepatitis B, poliomyelitis, meningococcal A and C, and rabies.
• A certificate of vaccination for yellow fever is required for anyone over 1 year of age and entering from an infected area.

OTHER HEALTH CONSIDERATIONS

• Water, food, and personal hygiene advice (including prevention of travellers' diarrhoea)
• Insect bite avoidance
• Avoidance of animal bites (to lessen the risk of rabies)
• Other hazards such as bilharzia
• Sun and heat precautions
• Accident risks (possibility of carrying a sterile medical pack)
• Risks associated with casual sex and prevention of blood-borne infections
• Full medical insurance

WEATHER – Kampala

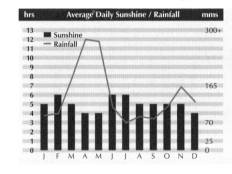

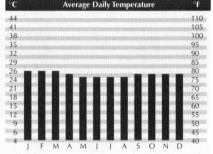

UKRAINE

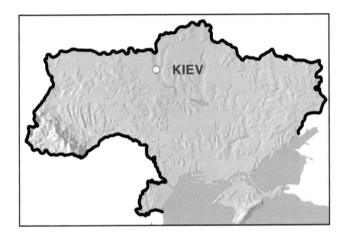

KIEV

OTHER HEALTH CONSIDERATIONS

- Water, food, and personal hygiene advice (including prevention of travellers' diarrhoea)
- Insect bite avoidance
- Avoidance of animal bites (to lessen the risk of rabies)
- Sun and heat precautions (in summer months)
- Accident risks (possibility of carrying a sterile medical pack)
- Risks associated with casual sex and prevention of blood-borne infections
- Full medical insurance

IMMUNISATION ADVICE

- Immunisations recommended in Britain should be up to date, especially those for children and tetanus boosters for adults.
- Courses or boosters of hepatitis A and diphtheria vaccines are usually advised.
- Vaccines sometimes recommended are: poliomyelitis, rabies, tuberculosis, hepatitis B, typhoid, and tick-borne encephalitis.

- No certificate of vaccination for yellow fever is required.
- Malaria is not normally present.

WEATHER – Kiev

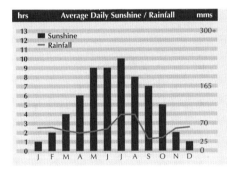

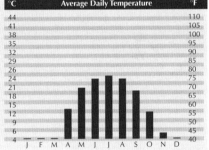

UNITED ARAB EMIRATES

MALARIA ADVICE

- Malaria is a serious and some-times fatal disease transmitted by mosquitoes. There is no vaccine available for malaria.

Malaria Precautions

- Malaria precautions are essential in the foothills and valleys of the mountainous regions of the north, all year round. The risk is very small in cities such as Dubai and Abu Dhabi. Avoid mosquito bites by covering up with clothing (long sleeves and long trousers) especially after sunset, using insect repellents on exposed skin, and, when necessary, sleeping under an impregnated mosquito net.
- Check with your doctor or nurse about suitable antimalarial tablets.
- Prompt investigation of fever is essential.

IMMUNISATION ADVICE

- Immunisations recommended in Britain should be up to date, especially those for children and tetanus boosters for adults.
- A course or booster of hepatitis A vaccine is usually advised.
- Vaccines sometimes advised are: poliomyelitis, diphtheria, tuberculosis, rabies, hepatitis B, and typhoid.
- No certificate of vaccination for yellow fever is required.

OTHER HEALTH CONSIDERATIONS

- Water, food, and personal hygiene advice (including prevention of travellers' diarrhoea)
- Insect bite avoidance (to reduce risk of dengue)
- Avoidance of animal bites (to lessen the risk of rabies)
- Sun and heat precautions
- Accident risks (possibility of carrying a sterile medical pack)
- Risks associated with casual sex and prevention of blood-borne infections
- Full medical insurance

WEATHER – Abu Dhabi

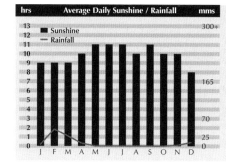

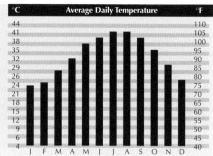

UNITED REPUBLIC OF TANZANIA

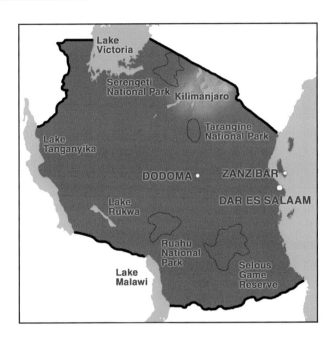

MALARIA ADVICE

- Malaria is a serious and sometimes fatal disease transmitted by mosquitoes. There is no vaccine available for malaria.

Malaria Precautions

- Malaria precautions are essential in all areas below 1,800 m, all year round. Avoid mosquito bites by covering up with clothing (long sleeves and long trousers) especially after sunset, using insect repellents on exposed skin, and, when necessary, sleeping under an impregnated mosquito net.
- Check with your doctor or nurse about suitable antimalarial tablets.
- Prompt investigation of fever is essential. A person travelling to remote areas should carry, for emergency, standby treatment.

IMMUNISATION ADVICE

- Immunisations recommended in Britain should be up to date, especially those for children and poliomyelitis and tetanus boosters for adults.
- Courses or boosters of diphtheria, hepatitis A, typhoid

and yellow fever vaccines are usually advised.
- Vaccines sometimes recommended are: poliomyelitis, tuberculosis, meningococcal A and C, hepatitis B, and rabies.
- A certificate of vaccination for yellow fever is required for anyone over 1 year of age and entering from an infected area.

OTHER HEALTH CONSIDERATIONS

- Water, food, and personal hygiene advice (including prevention of travellers' diarrhoea)
- Insect bite avoidance
- Avoidance of animal bites (to lessen the risk of rabies)
- Other hazards such as bilharzia
- Sun and heat precautions
- Accident risks (possibility of carrying a sterile medical pack)
- Risks associated with casual sex and prevention of blood-borne infections
- Full medical insurance

WEATHER – Dar es Salaam

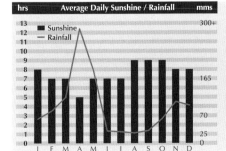

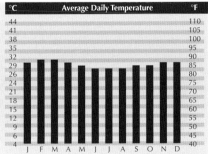

UZBEKISTAN

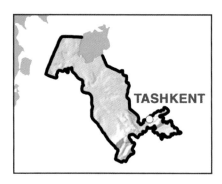

TASHKENT

IMMUNISATION ADVICE

- Immunisations recommended in Britain should be up to date, especially those for children and tetanus boosters for adults.
- Courses or boosters of diphtheria, hepatitis A and typhoid vaccines are usually advised.
- Vaccines sometimes recommended are: tuberculosis, rabies, hepatitis B, tick-borne encephalitis, and poliomyelitis.
- No certificate of vaccination for yellow fever is required.
- Malaria is not normally present.

OTHER HEALTH CONSIDERATIONS

- Water, food, and personal hygiene advice (including prevention of travellers' diarrhoea)
- Insect bite avoidance
- Avoidance of animal bites (to lessen the risk of rabies)
- Sun and heat precautions (in summer months)
- Accident risks (possibility of carrying a sterile medical pack)
- Risks associated with casual sex and prevention of blood-borne infections
- Full medical insurance

WEATHER – Tashkent

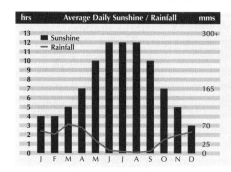

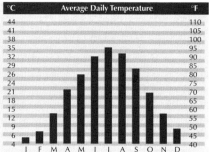

VENEZUELA (INCLUDING MARGARITA ISLAND)

MALARIA ADVICE

- Malaria is a serious and sometimes fatal disease transmitted by mosquitoes. There is no vaccine available for malaria.

Malaria Precautions

- Malaria precautions are essential in rural areas and Amazon regions, all year round. Risk is minimal in Caracus, Margarita Island, and the central coastal regions. Avoid mosquito bites by covering up with clothing (long sleeves and long trousers) especially after sunset, using insect repellents on exposed skin, and, when necessary, sleeping under an impregnated mosquito net.

- Check with your doctor or nurse about suitable antimalarial tablets.
- Prompt investigation of fever is essential. A person travelling to remote areas should carry, for emergency, standby treatment.

IMMUNISATION ADVICE

- Immunisations recommended in Britain should be up to date, especially those for children and tetanus boosters for adults.

- Courses or boosters of hepatitis A, typhoid and yellow fever vaccines are usually advised. (Yellow fever has not been reported recently on Margarita Island).
- Vaccines sometimes recommended are: tuberculosis, hepatitis B, diphtheria, and rabies.
- No certificate of vaccination for yellow fever is required.

OTHER HEALTH CONSIDERATIONS

- Water, food, and personal hygiene advice (including prevention of travellers' diarrhoea)
- Insect bite avoidance (to reduce risk of dengue)
- Avoidance of animal bites (to lessen the risk of rabies)
- Other hazards such as bilharzia
- Sun and heat precautions
- Accident risks (possibility of carrying a sterile medical pack)
- Risks associated with casual sex and prevention of blood-borne infections
- Full medical insurance

WEATHER – Caracas

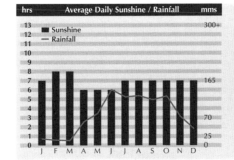

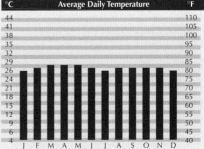

VIETNAM

MALARIA ADVICE

- Malaria is a serious and some-times fatal disease transmitted by mosquitoes. There is no vaccine available for malaria.

Malaria Precautions

- Malaria precautions are essential in rural border areas with Laos, Cambodia, and China all year round. The risk is minimal in major cities, the Red River delta, and the coastal plains of Nha Trang. Avoid mosquito bites by covering up with clothing (long sleeves and long trousers) especially after sunset, using insect repellents on exposed skin, and, when necessary, sleeping under an impregnated mosquito net.
- Check with your doctor or nurse about suitable antimalarial tablets.
- Prompt investigation of fever is essential. A person travelling to remote areas should carry, for emergency, standby treatment.

IMMUNISATION ADVICE

- Immunisations recommended in Britain should be up to date, especially those for children and tetanus boosters for adults.
- Courses or boosters of diphtheria, hepatitis A and typhoid vaccines are usually advised.
- Vaccines sometimes recom-mended are: tuberculosis, rabies, hepatitis B, Japanese B encephalitis, and poliomyelitis.

- A certificate of vaccination for yellow fever is required for anyone over 1 year of age and entering from an infected area.

OTHER HEALTH CONSIDERATIONS

- Water, food, and personal hygiene advice (including prevention of travellers' diarrhoea)
- Insect bite avoidance (to reduce risk of dengue)
- Avoidance of animal bites (to lessen the risk of rabies)
- Sun and heat precautions
- Accident risks (possibility of carrying a sterile medical pack)
- Risks associated with casual sex and prevention of blood-borne infections
- Full medical insurance

WEATHER – Ho Chi Minh City

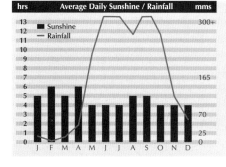

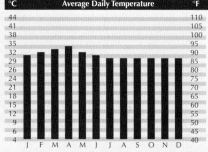

VIRGIN ISLANDS

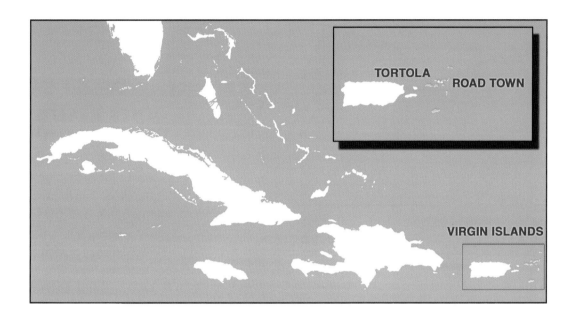

IMMUNISATION ADVICE

- Immunisations recommended in Britain should be up to date, especially those for children and tetanus boosters for adults.
- A course or booster of hepatitis A vaccine is usually advised.
- Vaccines sometimes recommended are: typhoid, diphtheria, hepatitis B, and tuberculosis.
- No certificate of vaccination for yellow fever is required.
- Malaria is not normally present.

OTHER HEALTH CONSIDERATIONS

- Water, food, and personal hygiene advice (including prevention of travellers' diarrhoea)
- Insect bite avoidance (to reduce risk of dengue)
- Avoidance of animal bites
- Sun and heat precautions
- Accident risks (possibility of carrying a sterile medical pack)
- Risks associated with casual sex and prevention of blood-borne infections
- Full medical insurance

WEATHER – Tortola

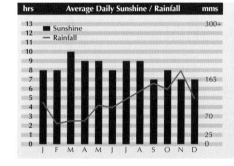

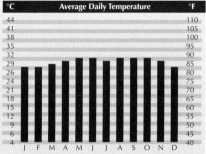

YEMEN

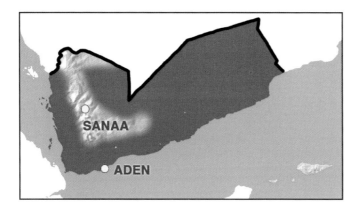

MALARIA ADVICE

- Malaria is a serious and some-times fatal disease transmitted by mosquitoes. There is no vaccine available for malaria.

Malaria Precautions

- Malaria precautions are essential in the whole country except Aden and the airport perimeter where the risk is minimal, all year round. Avoid mosquito bites by covering up with clothing (long sleeves and long trousers) especially after sunset, using insect repellents on exposed skin, and, when necessary, sleeping under an impregnated mosquito net.
- Check with your doctor or nurse about suitable antimalarial tablets.
- Prompt investigation of fever is essential. A person travelling to remote areas should carry, for emergency, standby treatment.

IMMUNISATION ADVICE

- Immunisations recommended in Britain should be up to date, especially those for children and tetanus boosters for adults.
- Courses or boosters of diphtheria, hepatitis A and typhoid vaccines are usually advised.
- Vaccines sometimes recommended are: poliomyelitis, tuberculosis, hepatitis B, and rabies.

WEATHER – Aden

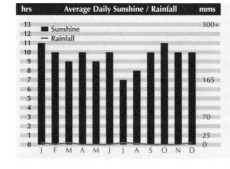

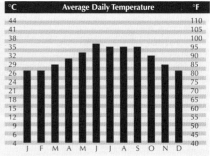

- A certificate of vaccination for yellow fever is required for anyone over 1 year of age and entering from an infected area.

OTHER HEALTH CONSIDERATIONS

- Water, food, and personal hygiene advice (including prevention of travellers' diarrhoea)
- Insect bite avoidance (to reduce risk of dengue)
- Avoidance of animal bites (to lessen the risk of rabies)
- Other hazards such as bilharzia
- Sun and heat precautions
- Accident risks (possibility of carrying a sterile medical pack)
- Risks associated with casual sex and prevention of blood-borne infections
- Full medical insurance

ZAMBIA

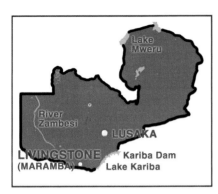

MALARIA ADVICE

- Malaria is a serious and sometimes fatal disease transmitted by mosquitoes. There is no vaccine available for malaria.

Malaria Precautions

- Malaria precautions are essential in all areas, all year round. Avoid mosquito bites by covering up with clothing (long sleeves and long trousers) especially after sunset, using insect repellents on exposed skin, and, when necessary, sleeping under an impregnated mosquito net.
- Check with your doctor or nurse about suitable antimalarial tablets.
- Prompt investigation of fever is essential. A person travelling to remote areas should carry, for emergency, standby treatment.

IMMUNISATION ADVICE

- Immunisations recommended in Britain should be up to date, especially those for children and tetanus boosters for adults.
- Courses or boosters of diphtheria, hepatitis A and typhoid vaccines are usually advised.
- Vaccines sometimes recommended are: poliomyelitis, tuberculosis, hepatitis B, rabies, yellow fever, and meningococcal A and C.
- A yellow fever vaccination is recommended for western districts, but there are no vaccine certificate requirements.

OTHER HEALTH CONSIDERATIONS

- Water, food, and personal hygiene advice (including prevention of travellers' diarrhoea)
- Insect bite avoidance
- Avoidance of animal bites (to lessen the risk of rabies)
- Other hazards such as bilharzia
- Sun and heat precautions
- Accident risks (possibility of carrying a sterile medical pack)
- Risks associated with casual sex and prevention of blood-borne infections
- Full medical insurance

WEATHER – Lusaka

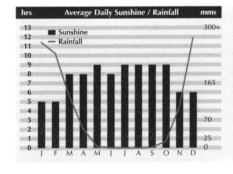

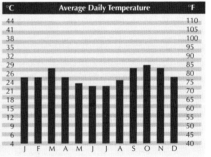

ZIMBABWE

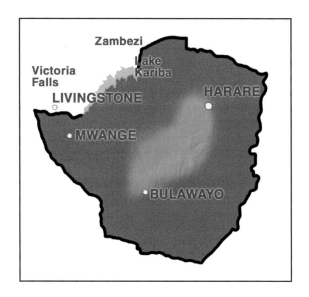

MALARIA ADVICE

- Malaria is a serious and sometimes fatal disease transmitted by mosquitoes. There is no vaccine available for malaria.

Malaria Precautions

- Malaria precautions are essential in the Zambezi Valley (including Victoria Falls) throughout the year and in all other areas below 1,200 m from November to June. Risk is small in areas above 1,200 m, including Harari. Avoid mosquito bites by covering up with clothing (long sleeves and long trousers) especially after sunset, using insect repellents on exposed skin, and, when necessary, sleeping under an impregnated mosquito net.
- Check with your doctor or nurse about suitable antimalarial tablets.

- Prompt investigation of fever is essential. A person travelling to remote areas should carry, for emergency, standby treatment.

IMMUNISATION ADVICE

- Immunisations recommended in Britain should be up to date, especially those for children and tetanus boosters for adults.

- Courses or boosters of diphtheria, hepatitis A and typhoid vaccines are usually advised.
- Vaccines sometimes recommended are: tuberculosis, hepatitis B, and rabies.
- A certificate of vaccination for yellow fever is required for anyone entering from an infected area.

OTHER HEALTH CONSIDERATIONS

- Water, food, and personal hygiene advice (including prevention of travellers' diarrhoea)
- Insect bite avoidance
- Avoidance of animal bites (to lessen the risk of rabies)
- Other hazards such as bilharzia
- Sun and heat precautions
- Accident risks (possibility of carrying a sterile medical pack)
- Risks associated with casual sex and prevention of blood-borne infections
- Full medical insurance

WEATHER – Harare

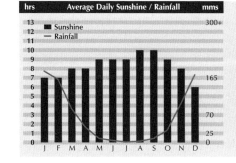

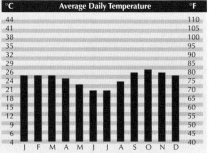